Perry Chen, Yancey Strickler, Charles Adler, and Kickstarter

INTERNET BIOGRAPHIES™

Perry Chen, Yancey Strickler, Charles Adler, and Kickstarter

DON RAUF

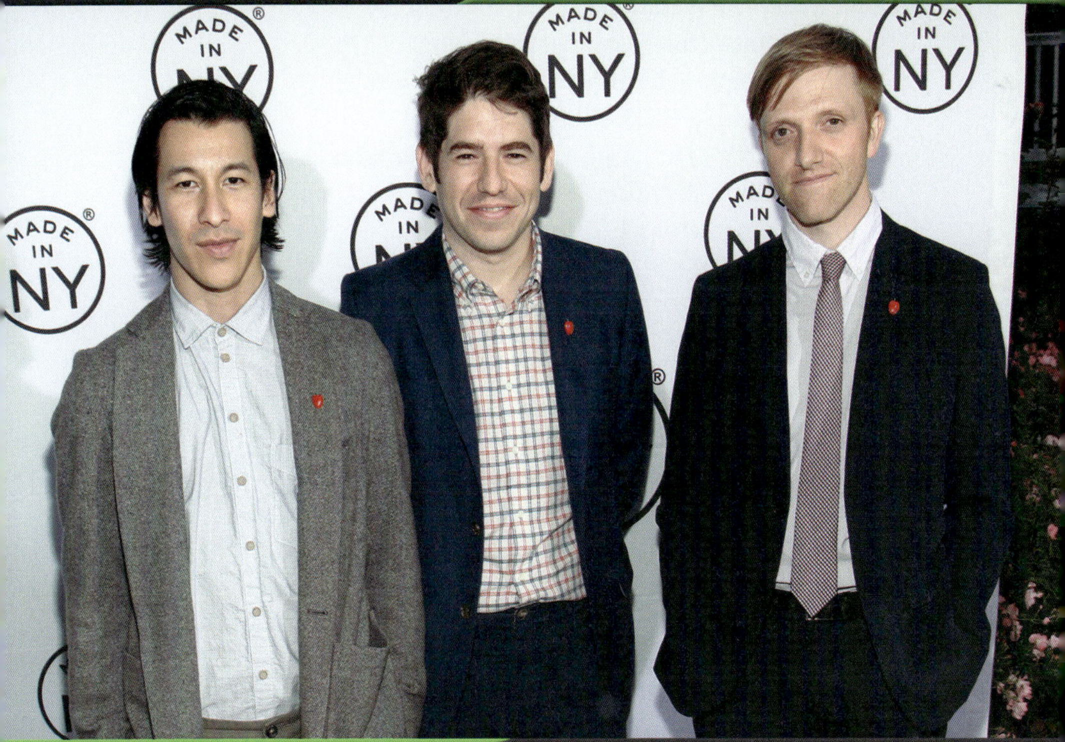

ROSEN PUBLISHING
New York

Published in 2014 by The Rosen Publishing Group, Inc.
29 East 21st Street, New York, NY 10010

First Edition

Library of Congress Cataloging-in-Publication Data

Rauf, Don.
Perry Chen, Yancey Strickler, Charles Adler, and Kickstarter/
Don Rauf.—First edition.
pages cm.—(Internet biographies)
Includes bibliographical references and index.
ISBN 978-1-4488-9523-6 (library binding)
1. Chen, Perry. 2. Strickler, Yancey. 3. Adler, Charles. 4. Venture capital. 5. Arts—Finance. 6. New business enterprises—Finance. 7. Internet marketing. I. Title.
HG4751.R38 2014
332'.041540922—dc23

2012039972

Manufactured in the United States of America

CPSIA Compliance Information: Batch #S13YA: For further information, contact Rosen Publishing, New York, New York, at 1-800-237-9932.

Contents

INTRODUCTION

Do you have an artistic project in mind? Many of us have such ambitions that we would like to make a reality. Some may be more eccentric than others. Usually the biggest factor holding us back from realizing a creative idea is money. That's where Kickstarter steps in.

Kickstarter is a Web site that helps people raise money to bring their creative dreams to life. The site relies on the concept of crowdfunding to finance entrepreneurial projects. When you crowdfund a project, you reach out to everyday people—friends, family, fans, and others—and ask them to donate toward your vision. They may contribute a very small amount or a very large sum, from $1 to $10,000. Through the power of the masses, small dollar amounts add up and creators can make their projects become a reality.

Amanda Palmer, a singer and songwriter known for her work with the Dresden Dolls, performs constantly and has developed a massive fan base around the globe. She used Kickstarter with the hopes of raising $100,000 to release an album with her new band, the Grand Theft Orchestra. She offered her fans gifts depending on the size of their donation. They ranged from a copy of the new record release to an art book to private shows for small groups of

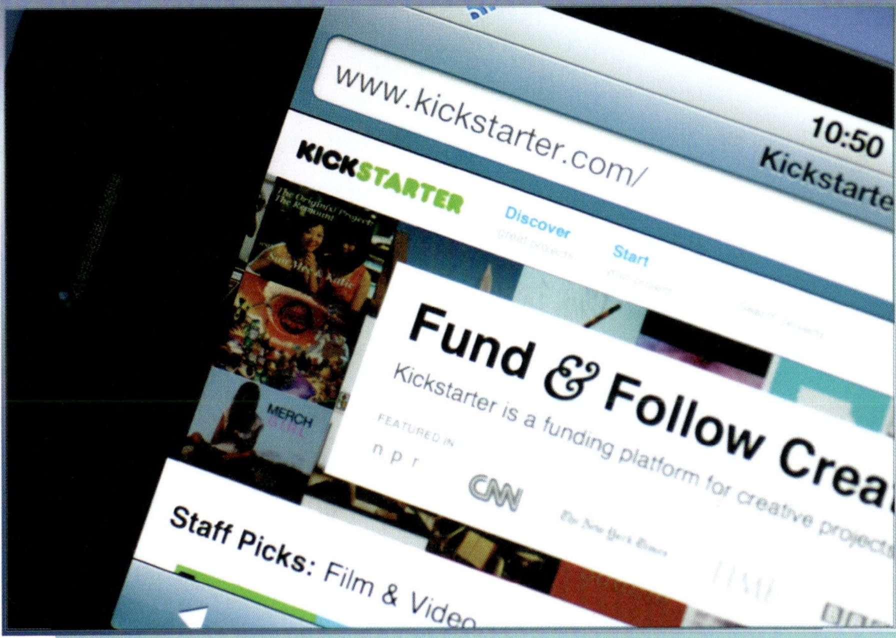

Kickstarter (www.kickstarter.com) helps people raise money to realize their creative projects. The site uses the idea of crowdfunding, where many people contributing small amounts can raise a lot of money.

supporters. Her rapport with her devout audience paid off beyond her wildest dreams. Palmer raised nearly $1.2 million from close to twenty-five thousand supporters.

The future of the music business, and crowdfunding, may be the future for all types of independent artists and innovators. Palmer disproved the idea that music fans will only download music for free. She showed that they will pay for music they believe in and feel a connection to.

The comedian Louis C. K. has also shown that crowdfunding is an effective way for supporting creativity. He self-financed a recording and production of his live comedy show. Although he didn't use Kickstarter, Louis C. K. offered the show for digital download via his Web site for $5. Within twelve days, he brought in more than $1 million. He did not have any middleman. Everything went directly from him to his fans. Seeing Louis C. K.'s success, comedian Aziz Ansari followed suit with a $5 digital download of one of his live shows.

The crowdfunding trend is on the rise, and it's changing the way people are doing business. The one Web site that is responsible for making it as popular as it is today is Kickstarter, founded by Perry Chen, Yancey Strickler, and Charles Adler.

Chapter 1

Kick-Starting Kickstarter

Perry Chen seemed like an unlikely person to start a groundbreaking, wildly popular online business. In 2002, Chen was unemployed and living in the French Quarter of New Orleans. The twenty-five-year-old was focused on creating original electronic music. He also enjoyed taking time to ride his bike around the city. As a music fan, Chen wanted to put on a big show with two up-and-coming deejays. The deejays were known for their remakes of pop and hip-hop songs.

The problem was that Chen's dream event would cost $15,000 to produce. When he thought about ways he could afford the show, he had to hope enough people would pay for admission at the door to cover the cost. He dropped the idea because he was afraid of going broke if no one showed up. He thought if he had had a plan to get people to pay for tickets in advance, he could have paid for the event without using any of his own money. He would have had no worries. He wondered if there was a way to turn his idea into a Web site.

THE SEEDS OF A SUCCESSFUL IDEA

Chen remembers standing in his kitchen talking to his roommate, Earl Scioneaux, about his Web site idea in late 2001 or early 2002. "I had been frustrated by my experience trying to put together a concert," Chen wrote on his blog. "The show never happened, but the idea for Kickstarter was born from my frustration."

Although he didn't act on the idea right away, he kept it in the back of his mind and moved on to other things. In 2005, he packed up his life in New Orleans and headed back to his hometown of New York City.

Arriving back in New York City, Chen felt that he needed something to do career-wise. He hadn't held down a steady job, so he thought most employers wouldn't hire him.

After searching around a bit, Chen landed a job waiting tables at a restaurant called Diner in the Williamsburg neighborhood of Brooklyn. This was and still is an area where a lot of young musicians and artists live. All the while, Chen kept his dream alive.

"The idea [for Kickstarter] stuck around in my head," Chen said on his blog. "Good ideas do that. Really good ideas call to you and remind you that they're there. Every so often I would wonder when someone else was going to do it. When a site like Kickstarter would just appear on the Web one day. It didn't happen."

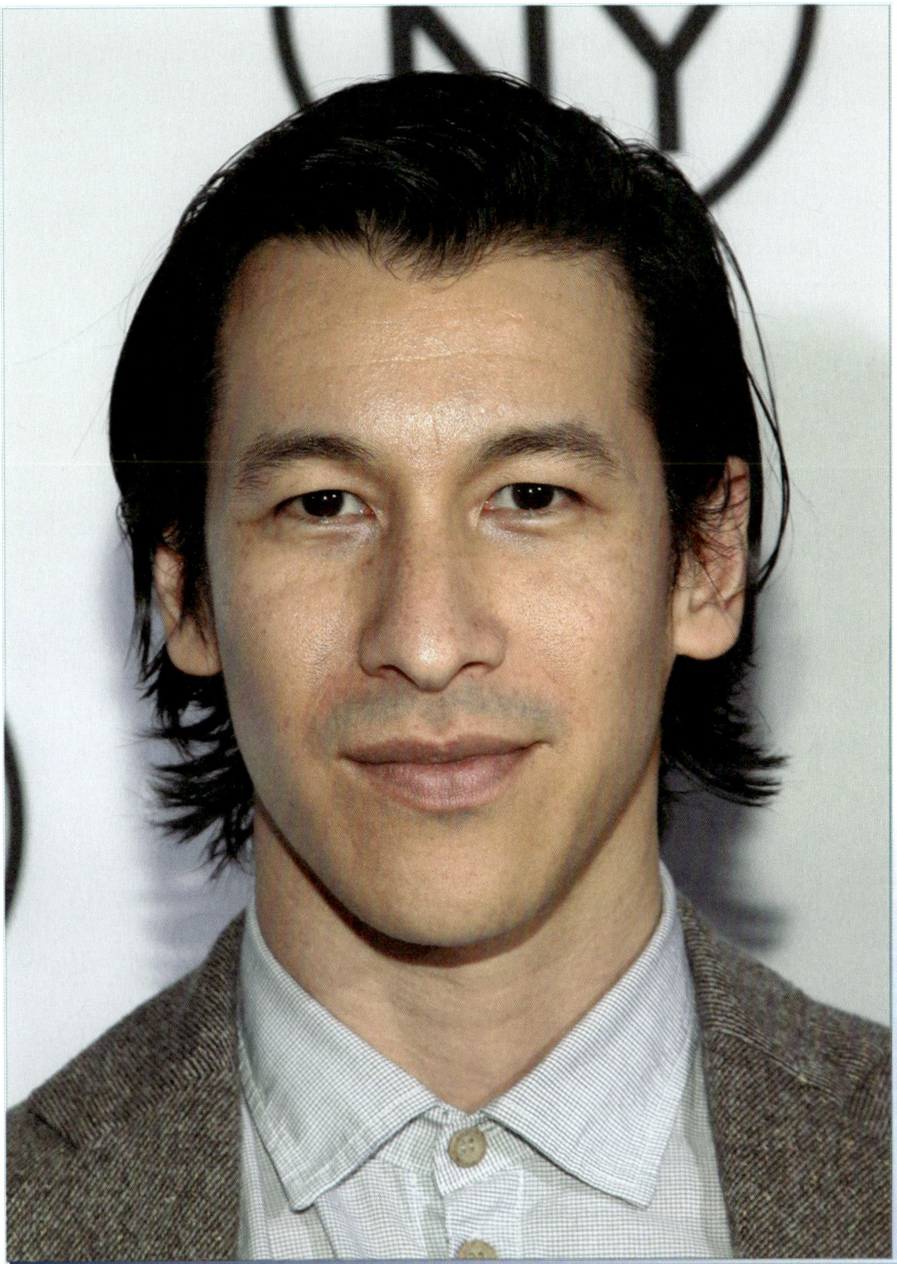

At age twenty-five, Perry Chen was interested in making electronic music. He seemed like an unlikely person to start a successful online business, but he had an idea for Kickstarter and he doggedly pursued it.

A FORTUNATE MEETING

Around the time that Chen moved back to New York City, Yancey Strickler was working as an editor and writer for eMusic, an online music business. The twenty-five-year-old Strickler frequently ate brunch at Diner, where Chen would often wait on him. Both Chen and Strickler were passionate about music, and they became friends.

In bits and pieces, Chen started to share with Strickler the idea he had about how to raise money in advance for artistic projects. Their personalities seemed to complement each other. Chen had a more nervous energy that seemed to come from his growing up in New York City. Strickler was more calm and laid back. He was born in Blacksburg, Virginia, and grew up

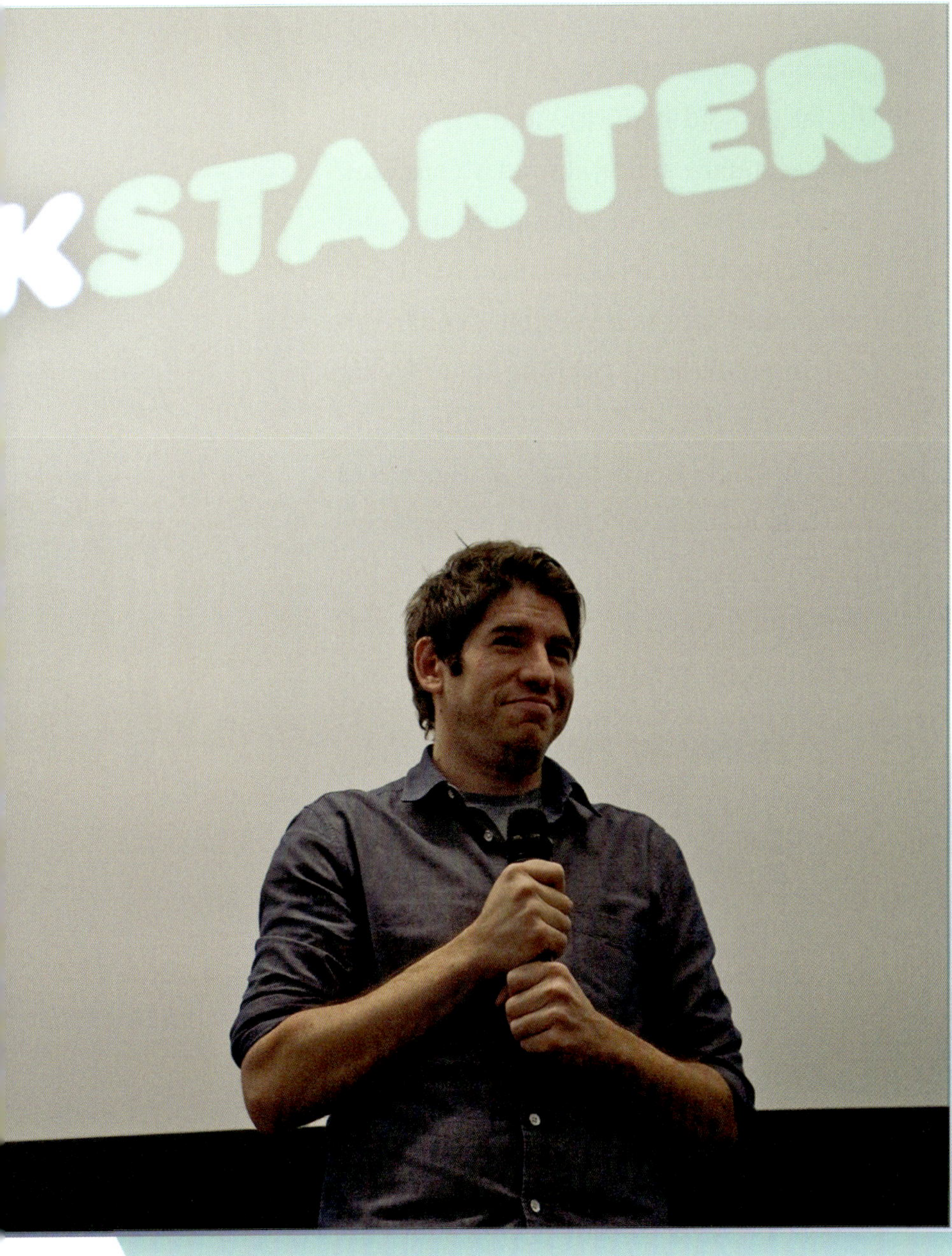

Before teaming with Perry Chen, Yancey Strickler was a music writer and an editor for eMusic, an online music business. Strickler's more laid-back personality balanced Chen's energy.

on a farm near a small town in the Appalachian Mountains called Newport. His father sold furniture and his mother was a secretary and is now an accountant. His stepfather is an auto mechanic and his stepmother sells real estate. As Strickler has said, it was a very blue-collar upbringing and there's nothing about it that would seem to lead him to where he is now.

Although neither one of them had any background in creating technology, Chen and Strickler agreed to pursue the idea and try to create a Web tool for raising money for creative projects.

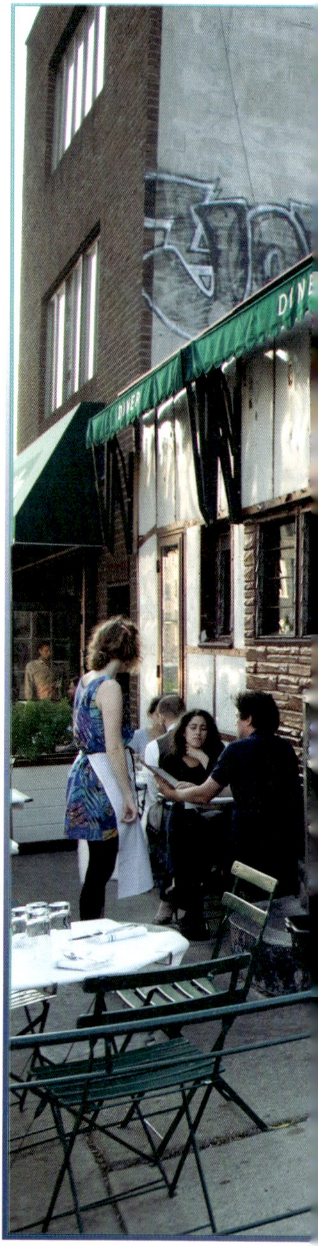

HONING THE IDEA

Chen and Strickler were both passionate about developing a Web tool that would help people realize their creative projects. They met and sketched out possible Web site ideas for a business.

Chen and Strickler honed their idea to a business that would allow people to fund projects they wanted to see come to life. They envisioned it as a tool that would let creators set the amount of funding they needed for a project. Strickler and Chen envisioned that creators

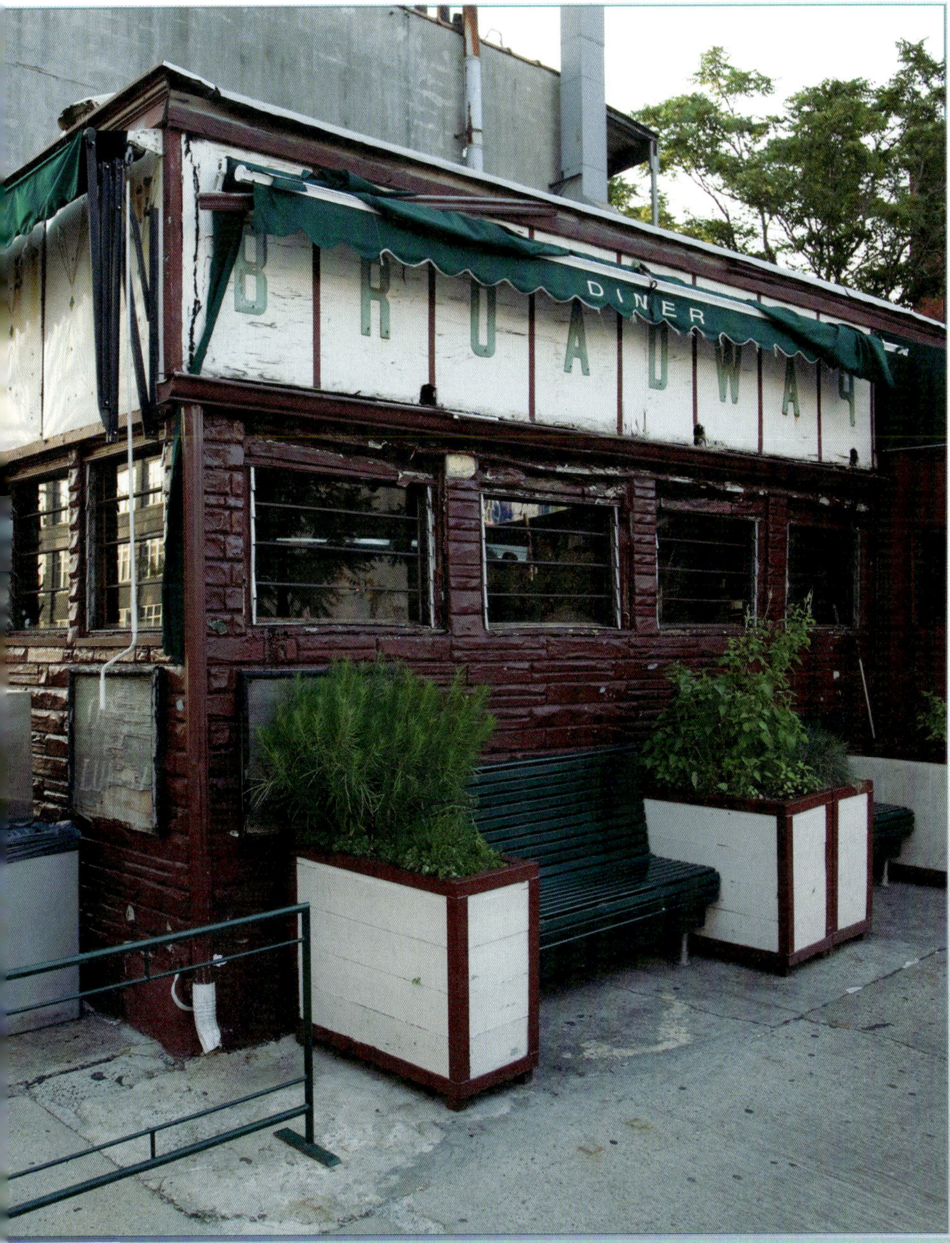

Yancey Strickler was a frequent customer at a restaurant called Diner where Perry Chen worked as a waiter. The two became friends, and Strickler joined forces with Chen to pursue his idea for a crowdfunding Web site.

would set a funding goal that would have to be met by a set deadline. If an artist met his or her money-raising goal or surpassed it by deadline, then contributors' credit cards would be charged and the artist would get cash.

FINDING THE RIGHT PERSON

To bring this idea to life, Strickler and Chen realized that they needed someone with a background in design, technology, and the Internet. In 2007, they met Charles Adler through a friend of a friend. Adler, who was thirty-eight years old, was a Web designer who had been working for Agency.com, an interactive marketing agency based in New York City. The company specialized in Web development and online marketing. Strickler and Chen asked Adler to help build the Web site's look and feel.

Since high school, Adler had been interested in design and architecture. He liked the idea of how functionality and design worked together. At Purdue University, Adler studied mechanical engineering, but he also took time to design posters for house parties. The Internet fascinated Adler, and he became intrigued by Web design. By 1995, he left college to work at an Internet design firm in Chicago. Although he had left school, his experience in engineering taught him the value of problem solving. Adler said that problem-solving skills were essential in developing Kickstarter. He has depended on

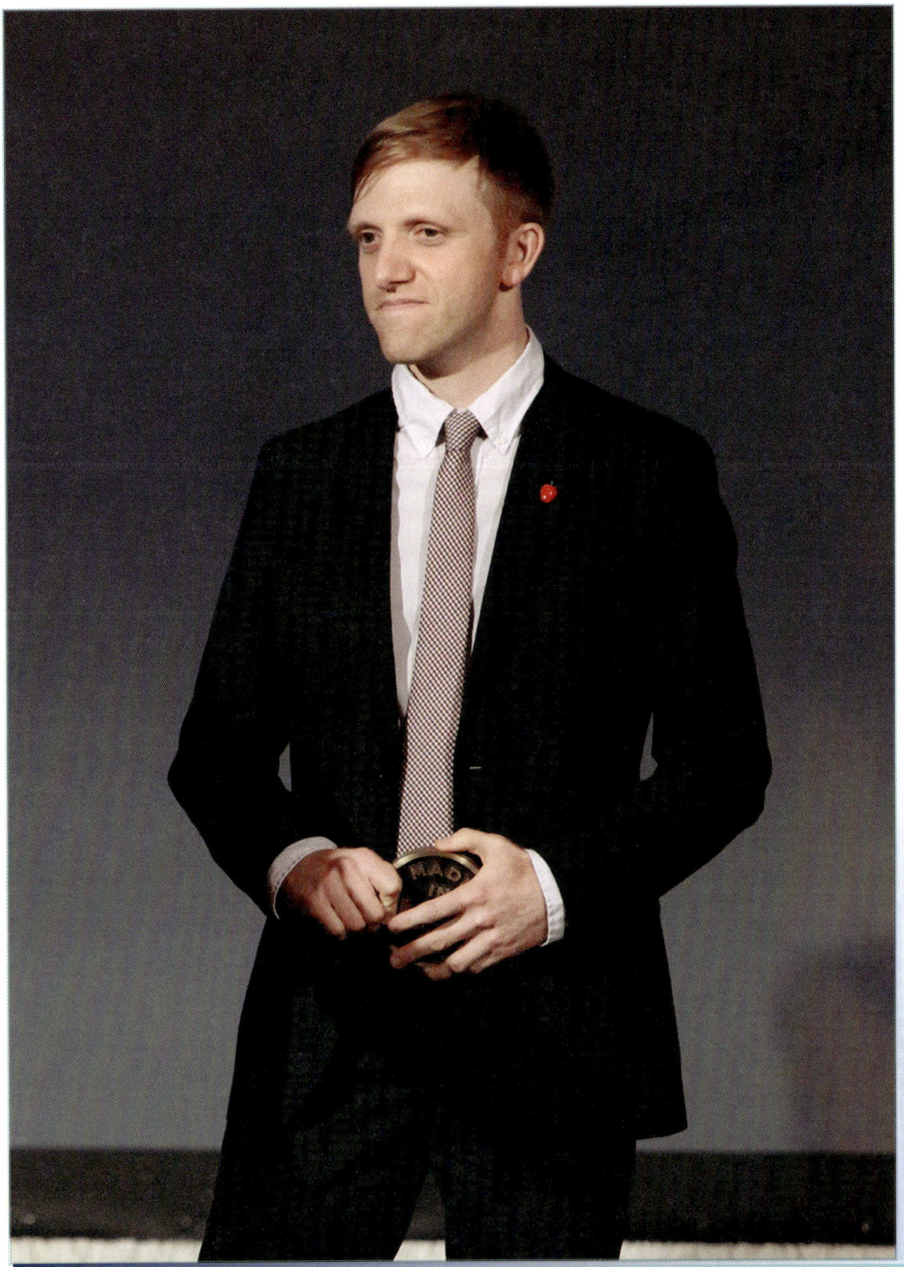

Charles Adler brought technical smarts to the creative team of Chen and Strickler. He worked on several Web site projects before joining the Kickstarter team.

this skill for design work and for all the details necessary for building a business.

Adler had an insatiable curiosity, and he was constantly interested in taking on new projects. Before joining the Kickstarter team, he traveled overseas and worked with several different teams on new Web site projects. A year before meeting Chen and Strickler, he opened his own small business. He was intrigued by the idea of building an Internet business like Twitter or WordPress.

Joining Chen and Strickler, Adler realized he was taking on the role of an entrepreneur. He said that starting your own business requires that you have a lot of confidence in your ability to execute your idea and that you're willing to accept a certain level of insanity.

"The cards are stacked against you in the most profound ways," said Adler in an interview on Subtraction .com. "There's never enough time or money, the majority of those around you tell you that what you're working on is illogical, and you never know enough at any given moment—at least in the early days, before a product gains traction or revenue. It's a leap of extreme faith."

Succeeding at bringing Kickstarter to life required patience, persistence, tenacity, and a level head, said Adler. "Sometimes a good idea is like an artifact that you find," wrote Chen on his blog. "It's deep in a cave, lodged in the earth, and you need people to help you pull it out and show the world."

A SLOW AND BUMPY ROAD AHEAD

Slowly, over the course of four years, the team moved forward with their concept. Chen kept other jobs to survive, including stock market trader and preschool teacher. To get Kickstarter launched properly, the team of Chen, Strickler, and Adler also needed seed money, or money to help them get started. Like many projects on Kickstarter, they turned to friends and family for help. Chen had a friend whose cousin is the comedian David Cross. Cross had starred on television's *Arrested Development* and in movies such as *Men in Black* and the Alvin and the Chipmunks series of films. He became an initial investor, along with Chris Kaski, the publisher of the music site Pitchfork.

Yet, Strickler remembers losing confidence as they crept toward launching. He felt that they might not be able to make their idea become a reality. At one point, Strickler said he had basically given up. Venture capitalists weren't interested. "It was not a happy period," said Strickler in an NPR interview.

Strickler said that there was a large emotional toll because he kept a full-time job while Chen and Adler were working full-time for no money to get the business going. That caused stress and tension.

In addition to the pains of getting the business together, another discouraging factor was the amount of competition. When they thought of the idea, Strickler and Chen

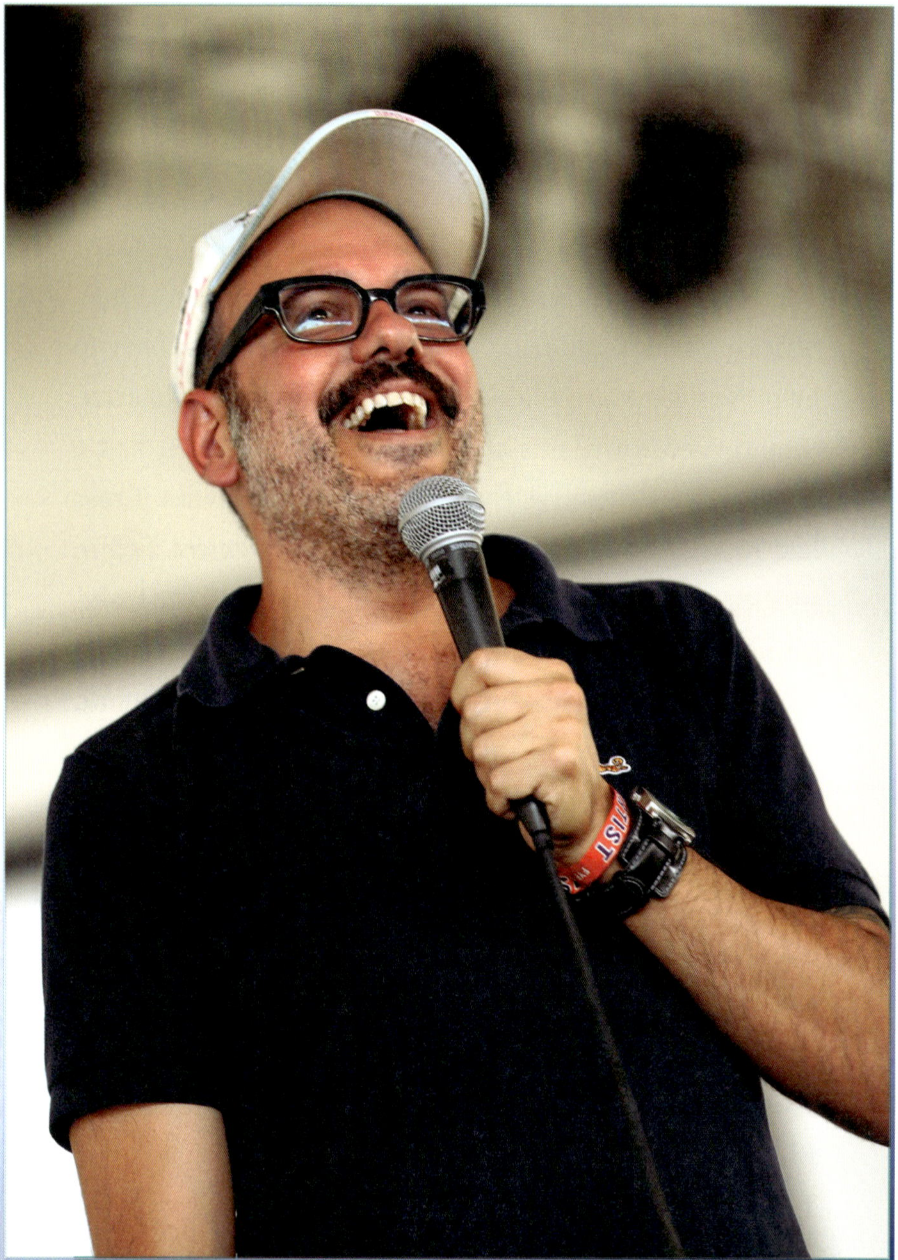

The comedian David Cross, who starred in the TV series *Arrested Development*, invested in Kickstarter early on. He was among a few family and friends who helped Kickstarter get off the ground when others had rejected the idea.

did not see any other similar businesses out there. Now, similar Web sites were launching. These sites were letting individuals make small donations to help fund projects. DonorChoose targeted teachers who were looking to raise money for classroom projects. Sellaband came along with its site for fans to fund music projects. Indiegogo was very similar to Kickstarter but accepted a wider variety of fund-raising projects, from liver transplants to dream weddings. Still, the team thought that their own design and vision was unique and that they could still make it work.

Looking back, Strickler said that these years before launching were helpful. During this time, they stripped down their idea to a very simple, focused tool. They figured out what the essence of Kickstarter should be and pushed that forward.

Strickler admits that getting Kickstarter off the ground was very hard and they made many mistakes. He said that they thought they could run the business with outside developers and workers, but they met with experienced businesspeople who told them that wouldn't work. In an interview on NPR, Strickler said that going to outside firms to write computer code was "the biggest mistake we made." Paying someone by the hour somewhere is different than having someone working in the room with you, living and breathing the project, said Strickler. When people are working as outside developers, your interests aren't aligned, he said. It makes it difficult.

Lessons Learned from Starting Up a Business

When a rock critic and a waiter decided to start a Web-based business, it may have seemed like their chances for success were fairly low. But now that their business is expanding rapidly, Yancey Strickler can look back and tell you that their success as tech entrepreneurs comes down to three lessons that can benefit anyone with a great business idea.

- If you don't succeed right away, don't give up. It took Chen and Yancey five years to make their initial idea a reality.
- Chance meetings can play a role in success. Get out there. Meeting the right people can mean everything when it comes to finding the right team and support needed to make a business a hit.
- You don't have to be a tech wizard to create a tech start-up. Yancey and Chen knew nothing about Web technology or writing code. But they knew how to find the right people and organize the right team to get the job done.

Each day they made it up as they went along, but Strickler said they had strong instincts about what was right and what was wrong.

MORE FORTUNATE CONNECTIONS

Eventually, things started to turn around for Kickstarter. They met Sunny Bates, a business networking professional who knew how to bring the right people together to start a business—executives, scientists, artists, creators, entrepreneurs, educators, philanthropists, and visionaries connect through her business. Bates focused on building meaningful partnerships for both companies and individuals. Strickler called her the "the most connected woman in New York" in an interview on the *Startups* Webcast.

Strickler said that Bates was a key to getting their business off the ground. And their meeting was another fortunate occurrence. Bates happened to live in the apartment building of a friend of Chen's. Chen's friend and Bates shared a dog walker. The friend introduced Chen to Bates, and Bates took the Kickstarter team under her wing. Bates was known as a force who could help people make powerful connections for more funding and talented people. Strickler said that Bates really helped kick-start Kickstarter. She introduced them to Caterina Fake, founder of Flickr and Hunch, and she introduced them to Andy Baio.

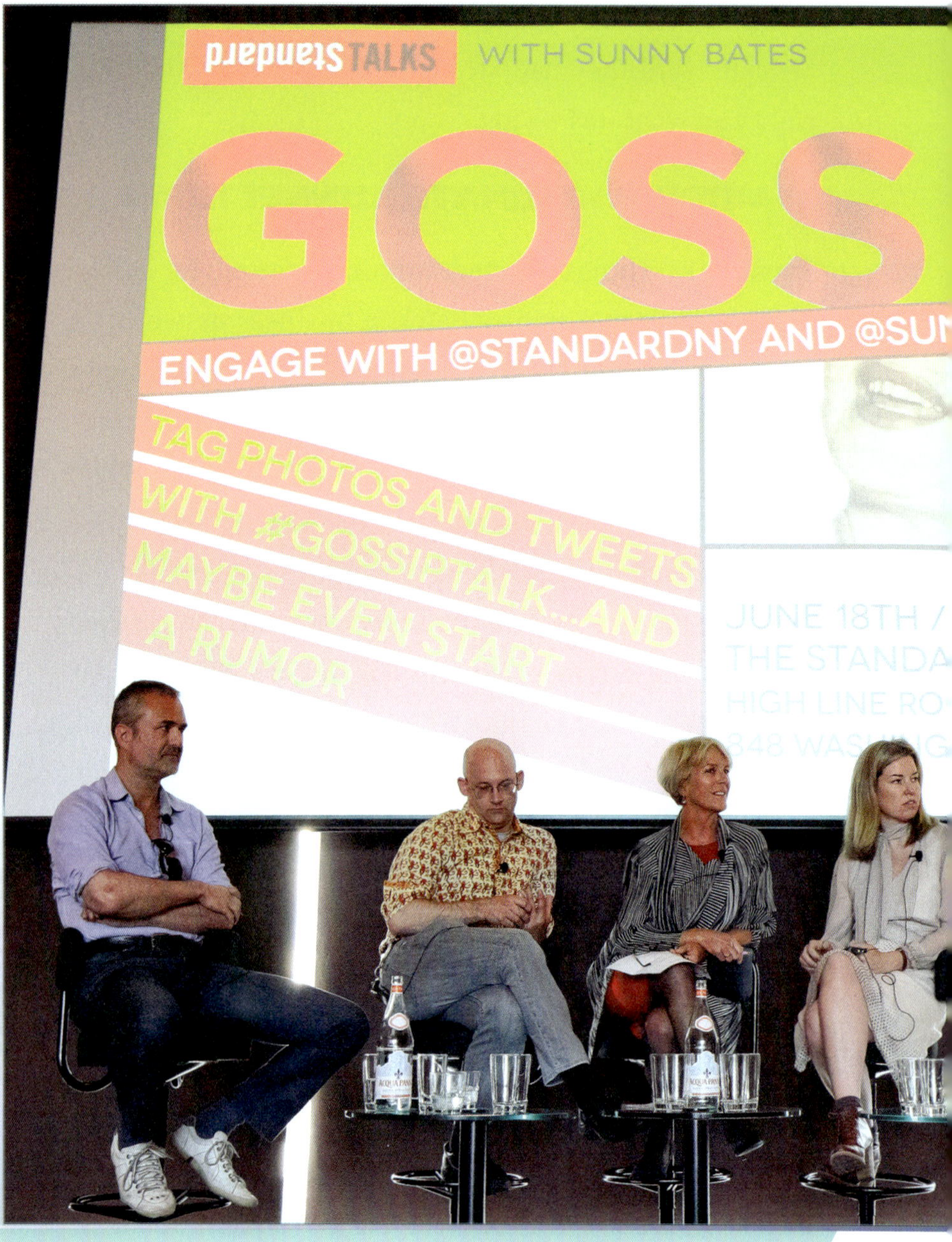

Chance connected Chen, Strickler, and Adler to Sunny Bates *(third from left)*. She is a business networking professional who led them to some crucial financial backers.

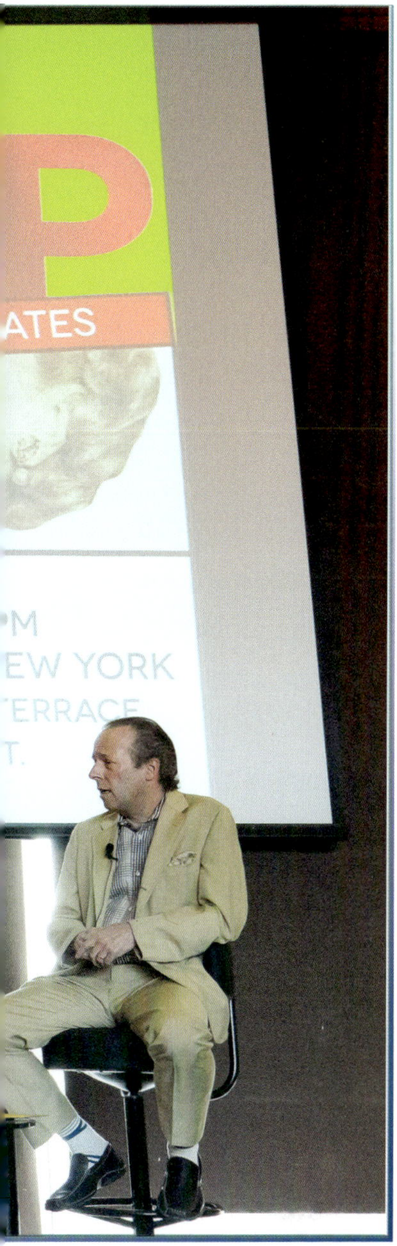

In 2008, Andy Baio, a tech entrepreneur in Portland, Oregon, joined the board of directors at Kickstarter. He had created a successful online creative event calendar in 2003 called Upcoming. Yahoo! bought his site and he worked for Yahoo! as a technical director until 2007. Baio made sure Kickstarter had the right technical plan in place. The team also hired three freelance developers in 2008. One was Lance Ivy, who was lured away from his home in Walla Walla, Washington, to become lead Web developer. As Strickler has said, a hard task for them was hiring the right technical talent, as they had no technical background themselves.

Over time, they rounded up more angel investors, including Caterina Fake, Twitter cofounder Jack Dorsey, Meetup cofounder Scott Heiferman, and Vimeo cofounder Zach Klein. They also received funding from venture capital firm Union Square Ventures. They raised a reported $10 million to really get the site going. "We have been lucky to make decisions based on our values and moral compass rather than chasing dollars," said Strickler in an interview with *Startups*.

A NEW WEB TOOL IS LAUNCHED

By 2008, the team had created models of their Web site, originally spelled "Kickstartr." They had already abandoned the name Critical Mass when they realized that the name was already taken.

But by fall of 2008, they had decided to go with the normal spelling of Kickstarter. In February 2009, the team now had a full working model—called an alpha version—of the site. They privately shared the site with a few friends to see what they thought.

On Tuesday, April 28, 2009, they launched the site for real. They invited their musician, artist, and photographer friends to join and they asked them each to invite five more people, and it gradually took off.

The funding platform attracted people with a range of creative projects, including films, recordings, photography, design, and comics. Many of the projects were—and still are—small. Strickler said that creators and those who give money love it because the projects come to the public without an intermediary, such as a bank or record label.

Kickstarter supports a lot of creative ideas that are not big moneymakers. If you have an idea for something you want to make happen, Kickstarter provides the tool to help you realize your vision. Strickler said that funding creative projects worked differently when they first started on the Kickstarter concept. Artists would get money through traditional methods like record labels, film studios, or publishers. "Those places are really looking for things that will be hits and what that means is that anyone that doesn't really fit that preconception of what a popular work could be is ignored," said Strickler in an interview on the game Web site PurplePawn.com. "So we wanted to create a space where an idea could exist just because you wanted it to and where communities would have a say in bringing what comes to life."

Three years later, Kickstarter is helping fund thousands of projects, generating millions of dollars in funding. And the business has also given the former waiter Chen something he never had before: a steady job.

Chapter 2

How Crowdfunding Works

The idea of getting other people to pay for artistic projects is not new. The popular thinking has been that artists need financial support from others so they can dedicate themselves to their art. Without financial resources, artists have to work for a living and cannot devote the time they need to their artistic endeavors.

Originally, the arts were supported by rich backers or patrons. The word "patron" in Latin means "one who gives benefits to his clients." Throughout history, patronage has been tied to monarchies and a well-off aristocracy—not just in Europe but in Asia as well. Feudal Japan, for example, cultivated a culture where the arts flourished.

In sixteenth century Florence, the wealthy Medici family kick-started the Italian Renaissance, a period when art of all different types flourished. They gave a vast fortune to support artists. Perhaps the most famous artists funded by the Medicis were Leonardo da Vinci and Michelangelo, but the family also gave money to others, such

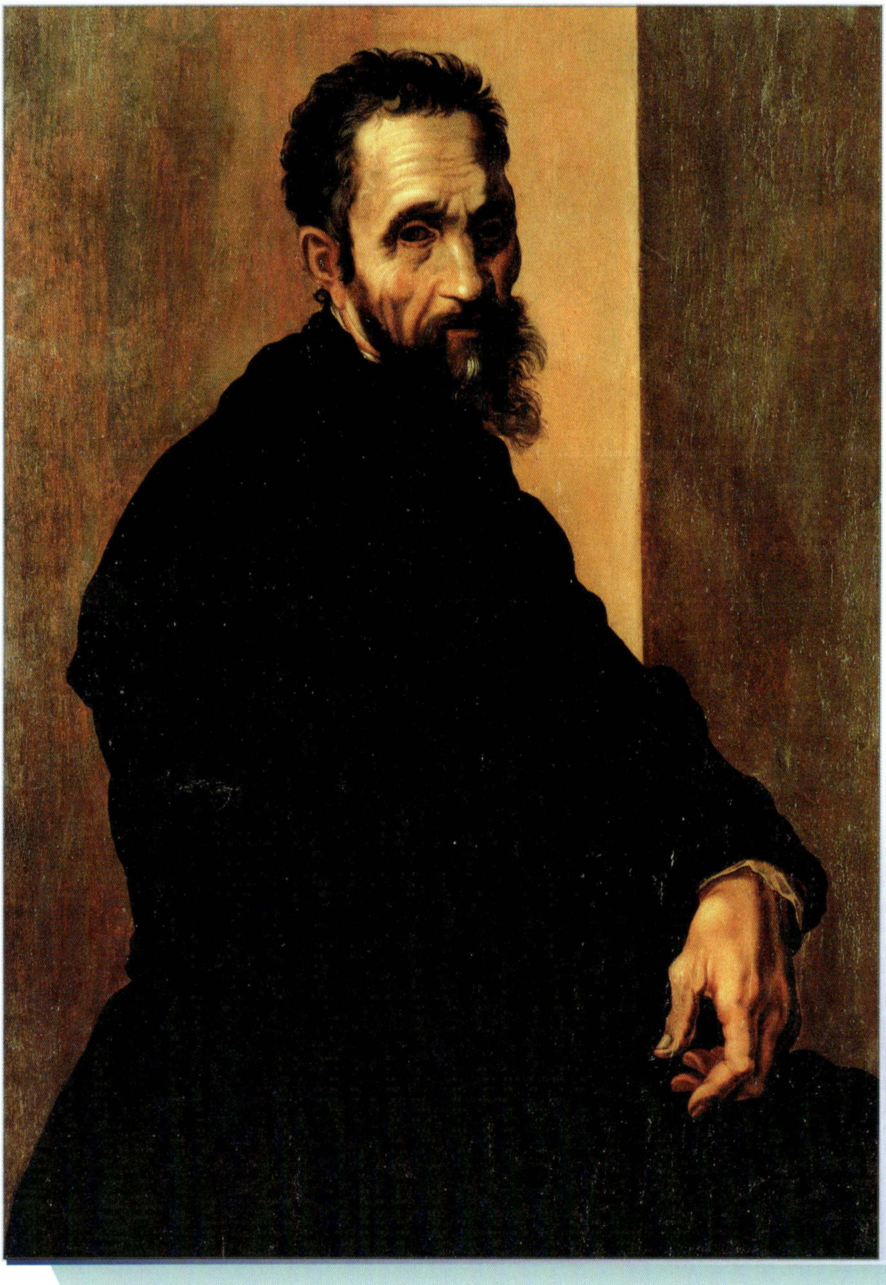

The idea of people giving money to support creative projects is not new. In the sixteenth century, the wealthy Medici family supported many artists, including Michelangelo. The artist is pictured here in a portrait by Jacopino del Conte.

as Boticelli, Fra Filippo Lippi, and Giambologna, the author Machiavelli, and various playwrights and composers. The Medicis funded Europe's first artist academy, many architectural works, fountains, sculptures, tapestries, music festivals, and operas.

In the seventeenth century, the authors William Shakespeare and Ben Jonson sought and enjoyed the support of noble patrons. Since the French Revolution, the Rothschild family has been a renowned patron to the arts. Composers Chopin, Mendelssohn, and Liszt all performed in the Rothschild home. Governments have also acted as patrons to the arts. Impressionist artists Henri Matisse and Paul Gaugin received financial support from the French government.

Andrew Carnegie, who had worked his way up from a poor Scottish immigrant to become a titan of the steel industry by the beginning of the twentieth century, donated hundreds of millions of dollars to support libraries, charities, and the arts.

Even this idea of crowdfunding through smaller contributions has been around for a long time. At the turn of the nineteenth century, Beethoven would perform many of his symphonies and have the donor's name printed on the program. Walt Whitman published some of his books in the exact same way. In the front of the book, he'd list all the people who helped him pay for his first run of printing.

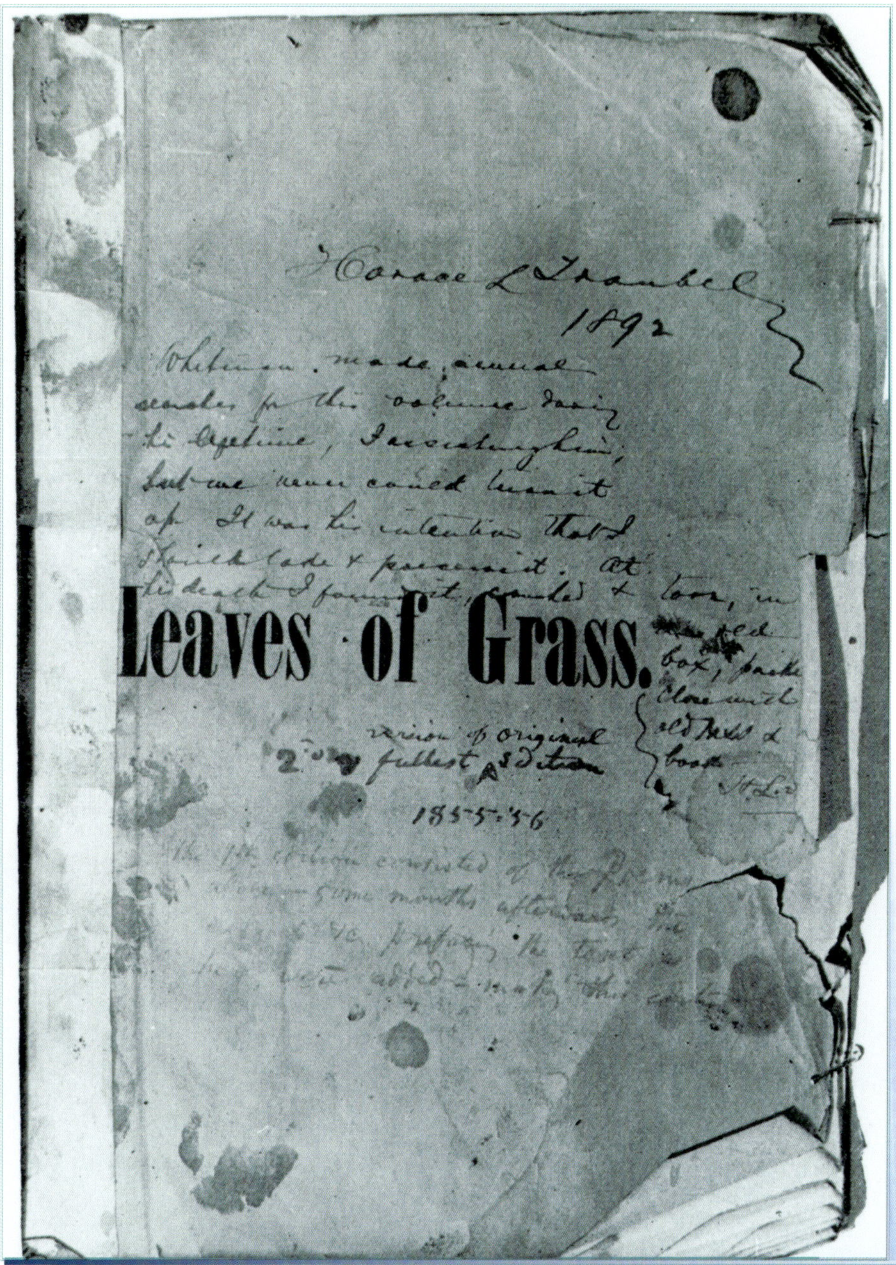

Poet Walt Whitman was an early crowdfunder. The author of *Leaves of Grass* relied on contributions from many people to fund first-run printings of some of his books.

As capitalism thrived throughout the twentieth century, governments and corporations poured money into public art projects—museums, symphonies, and opera companies. Yet, this type of goodwill has been shrinking in the past few decades. The annual budget for the National Endowment for the Arts was estimated at approximately $146 million for 2012. Kickstarter projects were expected to surpass that amount with an anticipated $150 million in financial backing for 2012. While Yancey Strickler recognizes that it would be great if this federal endowment had more money for supporting the arts, he sees Kickstarter as basically doubling the amount of funding available to the arts.

The fact that microgivers are giving more to support the arts than the U.S. government shows how the world of arts patronage continues to evolve. Artists have always depended on this patronage to flourish, but now more funding appears to be coming from individuals of more modest means than from corporations, governments, or even wealthy supporters.

ART FOR ART'S SAKE

Getting artistic endeavors off the ground can be difficult. It is tough to get a record label or movie studio to invest in most projects unless there was going to be a return on investment. Strickler said on a Tumblr post that Kickstarter was a way to break beyond the traditional methods of raising money, such as loans, investments, industry deals, and grants. By reaching out to individuals they know, artists could ask for small contributions. Additionally, each person who contributed would feel they had a stake in the project. Each project would build its community of contributors. And the goal would not be about making a profit. The goal would be creation—bringing a vision to life. Sometimes, people who don't know anything about a Kickstarter project donate funds. They browse the Web site and find projects that interest them and then give money, even if they don't know the creators at all.

The lifeblood of Kickstarter is social media, according to Strickler. He estimates that Kickstarter is mentioned on Twitter every eight seconds, and this informs people of creative endeavors that may inspire them to pull out their credit cards.

Projects that receive a lot of these donations are ones that Kickstarter highlights on its blog or picks as its "Projects We Love" in a weekly e-mail newsletter. Often these projects are picked based on the promotional materials submitted by the creator. The team appreciates an interesting video pitching the project and unique incentives for givers. Their first thought is usually, "Will this engage the audience?"

FUNDAMENTAL FUND-RAISING

A unique part of Kickstarter's setup is that the person raising the funds has to set a target amount that is needed to bring the idea to life. The creator must also set a length of time for raising the money. An average length is about a month. The maximum time for raising funds is ninety days. Kickstarter says that people get tired of a project if it's posted for too long. If the funding goal is not met, the person does not get the money. The idea behind this was that if the target amount couldn't be reached, then there wasn't enough interest in the project. The people who did pledge money do not get charged. Kickstarter does not receive any funds in this case, and the creators are not penalized for falling short of their goals. So raising money on Kickstarter is an all-or-nothing proposition.

While it may seem like an easy way to gather money for a creative endeavor, Strickler said that 54 percent of all projects launched on the Web site fail to meet their goal.

GIFTS FOR THE GIVERS

In addition to feeling like they're part of the project, contributors get something back. Creators offer incentives, which are gifts or tokens of appreciation. If you are an independent band, you might offer contributors a copy of the CD you produce. If you're an author or comic book artist, you might give a copy of the book you're writing to those who donate $10. Incentives have also included T-shirts and homemade objects. Incentives increase with the amount of donation—large donations may be rewarded with the opportunity to sing background vocals on a song, have a private show, or get a walk-on role in a movie being filmed.

FIRST PROJECTS OUT OF THE GATE

At the very beginning, Kickstarter needed to populate its site with projects. Strickler and Chen knew lots of friends who were artists, photographers, and musicians, and they reached out to them first. They used an invitation-only approach. They gave friends access to the site and asked them to invite five more people. Very quickly, the team saw demand for their service. People contacted them through the customer service section of the site, asking to post their ideas.

Their very first Kickstarter funding opportunity was a T-shirt project. It was not a success, raising $625 of its targeted $1,000. On May 3, 2009, the team had its very first hit—Drawing for Dollars. An artist was trying to raise a targeted $35. For $5, the artist would take an idea of yours, draw it, color it, and send you the art. He met his goal with three backers donating. An offline Wikipedia app raised $145. Soon after, the Kickstarter founders launched "New York Makes a Book," which asked people to contribute photos, art, and stories for a publication. The book raised $3,329 from 110 backers.

In the first month of business, Allison Weiss, a musician from Athens, Georgia, set out to raise $2,000 in

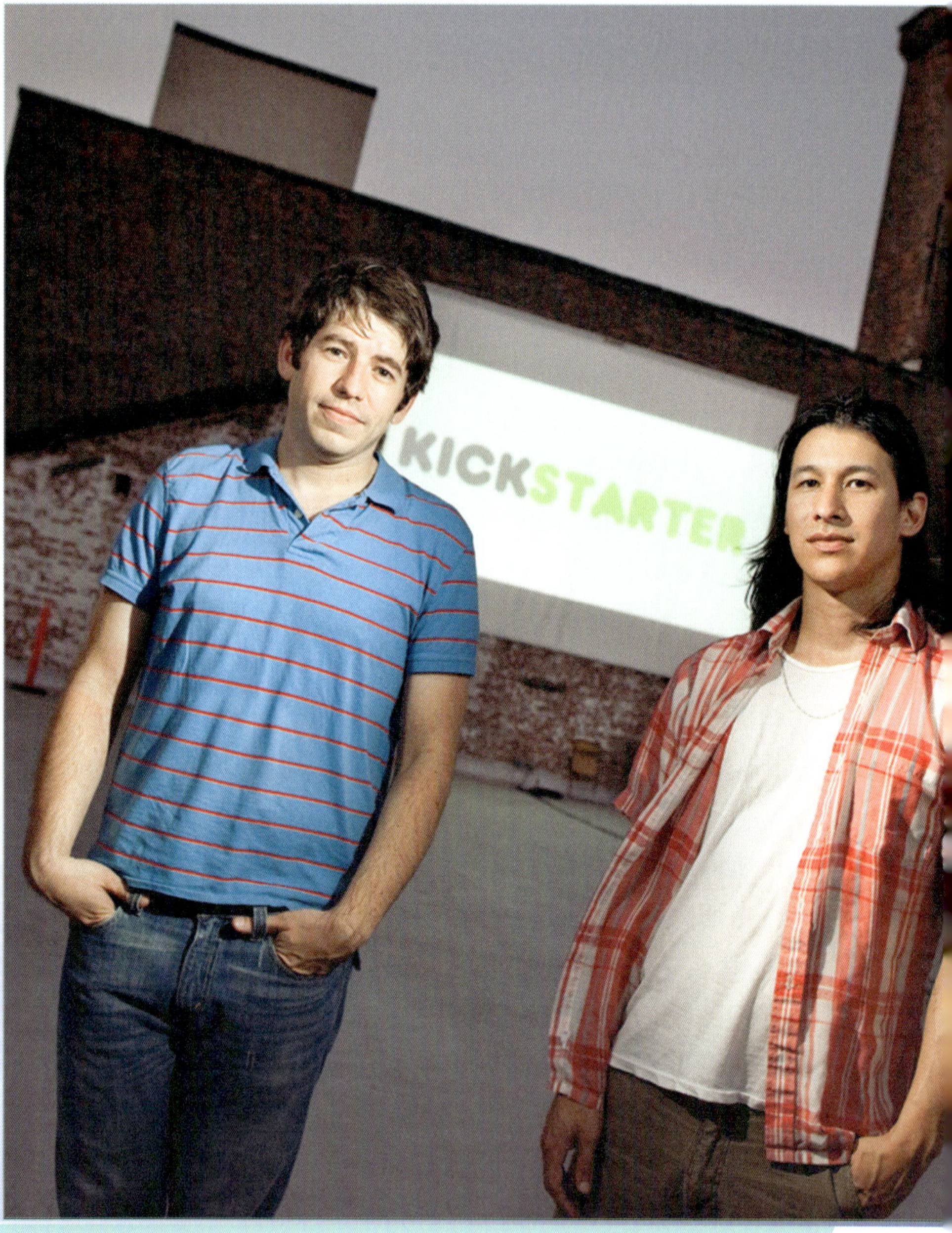

You can tell by the way that Strickler and Chen dress that Kickstarter has a casual work atmosphere. No ties and jacket here. A big loft space has served as headquarters for years.

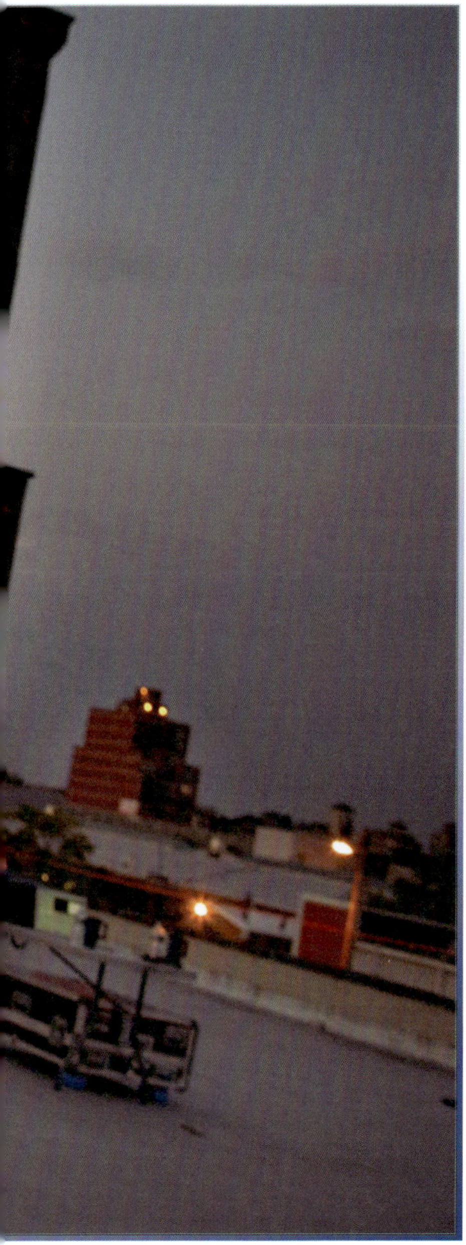

sixty days to make an EP of her music. In the end, she raised $7,711. Chen and Strickler still point to her as the model for how to make a small creative project work. She made a down-to-earth, funny video pitching to potential donors, holding up handmade signs giving reasons why they should give.

Emily Richman, an artist from Los Angeles, was sailing around the world alone and she raised money by telling people that if they sent in $15, she would send a Polaroid of a port from one of her locations. At some point on her trip, she mailed a photo to each of her supporters. She sent a map showing where she was and a letter telling about her journey. She raised about $7,500. For Yancey Strickler, this is the type of project that Kickstarter was designed to back.

What's It Like to Work at Kickstarter?

During its short history, Kickstarter headquarters has been located behind a graffiti-covered door in a converted three-floor walkup apartment in an old tenement building on Rivington Street on Manhattan's Lower East Side. There is no sign out front, so you wouldn't know that this tech company is humming along behind that nondescript door. In a big loft space that in many ways resembles a college dorm, a staff of about forty attend to the business, sitting behind their computer terminals. About half of the staff works on coding and designing, and half work with the community.

In the open space with sprawling tables and tin ceilings, much of the staff combs through proposals. On an average day, they get three hundred proposals, but on some days it can skyrocket to four times that number. Their goal is to respond to each proposal within twenty-four hours—occasionally it can take up to a week to get a response.

The atmosphere is relaxed, youthful, and low-key. No one comes to work wearing ties and jackets. From the plain blond wood floors to the original big windows, this is a no-frills atmosphere. They have a huge sign that says "PONG," which came from a

Ping-Pong club that was funded using Kickstarter, and they have a Ping-Pong table where workers take breaks. Strickler has said that it doesn't feel like work very often.

Kickstarter may be on the move, however. In the summer of 2012, the team purchased a landmark building in Brooklyn where it plans to move and have a rooftop garden.

HAVING A PERSONAL STAKE

When people contribute in this way, it is not considered investing. There is no equity or financial return. In an interview on NPR, Strickler said that we're all uncomfortable talking about money, and for artists in particular it's a very difficult issue. But the platform for Kickstarter makes it easy to donate. Also, by posting a project on Kickstarter, it's telling the world that the project is real. It is official. Although artists tell their friends, family, and fans to give money through the site, it's not like directly asking them to give money.

Joan Grossman, a documentary film director based in Brooklyn, raised $21,634 for her recent film *Drop City*, about a commune that was popular in Colorado during the 1960s. Grossman feels that asking people directly for money is very different than having them go through the intermediary of Kickstarter. Plus, donors have a real sense of inclusion. They feel like they are part of the project and the process. They feel some ownership and often some bragging rights if it succeeds.

In the *New York Times*, Patrick Rooney, director of research at the Center on Philanthropy at Indiana University, said that young donors with limited resources may find Kickstarter's model especially appealing. They don't have to be a wealthy donor to help the arts. "It's very personal in some ways, as opposed to giving a gift to, say, Indiana University," he said in the article.

The format provided by Kickstarter makes it easy to describe the project in detail. Creators can post videos showing what they're setting out to accomplish. They may outline how exactly the money will be spent and what they hope to accomplish. They can explain the origins of the project. If donators have questions about the project, supporters can post a question directly to the creator.

WHAT GETS THE THUMBS DOWN

Can any project get funded on Kickstarter? The answer is no. The staff at Kickstarter has to review the project first and approve it before it can go live. The project has to be creative, and for the team at Kickstarter, that's a broad definition. Still, many projects get the thumbs down. The projects also have to have an end point.

The stock answer to what won't get supported by Kickstarter is an idea such as "Buy Jenny a New Prom Dress." Charitable fund-raising and medical and health care–related causes are also barred, and Chen and his team are not going to help any major corporations launch a new product.

As Kickstarter grows, more projects will probably get rejected. Celebrated author Margaret Atwood set about to raise funds for an electronic pen that would allow authors to provide actual autographs to readers thousands of miles away. The idea was nixed by the Kickstarter team. In another instance, a blog described the experience of a woman who wanted to fund a stuffed animal pattern that a buyer could sew and put together. She said the idea was rejected by Kickstarter with no clear explanation as to why. Ross Fletcher has a humorous Web site dedicated to his "rejected" Kickstarter ideas, including vitamin beer, squid ink pens, and diapers designed to dust floors as the baby creeps about.

Chapter 3

A Boost for the Arts

Although more than 50 percent of Kickstarter projects do not meet their targeted goals and do not get launched, thousands of creative endeavors do get funded and meet their financial goals. In its short history, Kickstarter has been vital for many artists whose projects may never have seen the light of day if it were not for crowdfunding. In fact, the greatest number of successful Kickstarter projects are in dance, theater, music, and art.

A COMIC BOOK SMASH

You might not think that a comic book could be one of the biggest money-raisers, but a comic was the third project in the history of Kickstarter to break through the $1 million barrier. Cartoonist Rich Burlew has a Web-based comic called *Order of the Stick (OOTS)*. In 2002, Burlew began drawing the comic, which lovingly satirizes role-playing games and medieval fantasy—the setting closely

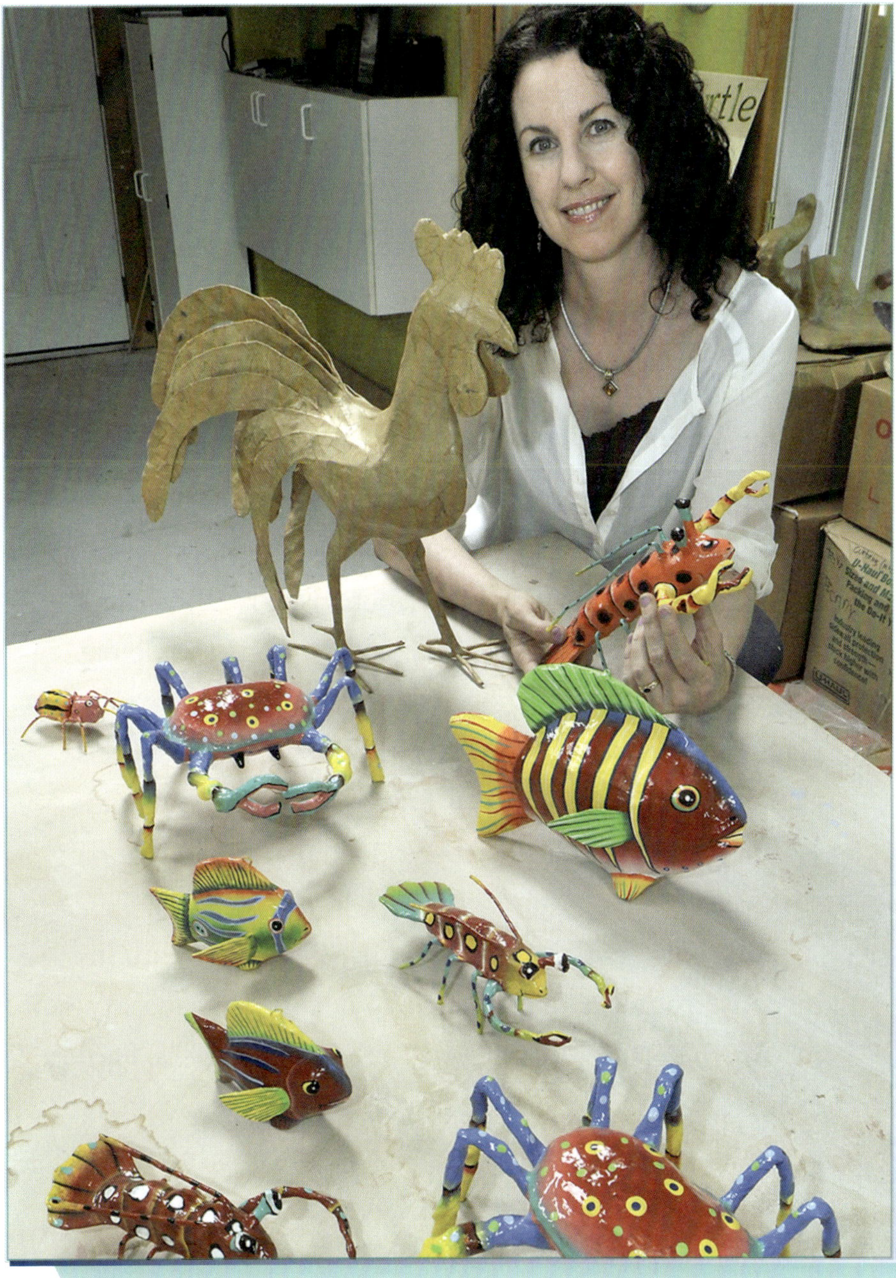

Artist Laura Bruzzese sells papier-maché creations from artists in Haiti on the Web site Etsy. She got funding to start her partnerships with Haitian artists through a Kickstarter campaign.

resembles *Dungeons and Dragons*. It's drawn in a lively, colorful but very simple stick-figure style.

Basically, the storyline is about six adventurers who are trying to save the world from an evil sorcerer named Xykon. Burlew was a fantasy game fanatic himself, and he began the cartoon on his Web site, where he wrote articles about gaming. He started it as a twice-weekly comic that appeared on Mondays and Thursdays. When he released a compilation book of the first *OOTS* comics, demand was so great that Burlew was able to make writing the comic his full-time job, and he produced three strips per week.

What makes one project more well-received than another is hard to say. Some believe *OOTS* is so popular because it caters to a dedicated audience of fantasy role-playing game fans. Kevin LaPorte and Amanda Rachels created a comic called *Clown Town*, and they've had modest success raising a few thousand dollars in funds on Kickstarter.

But Burlew is also credited for being clever with his incentive packages to get people to donate. He had sixty-four distinct packages for pledges at different levels. Each time he met a new goal during the drive, Burlew set another new goal and offered new incentives. Incentives included a sticker set, a magnet, card sets, coloring books, and more installments of the Webcomic.

For $10, donors could receive an *Order of the Stick* fridge magnet and a digital PDF of the original comic.

Those who gave $100 could get four magnets; $200 got you books, prints, and autographs; $600 equaled an original crayon drawing by Burlew. Big-money backers who gave $5,000 won a cameo in the *Order of the Stick* Webcomic. In the end, Burlew raised over $1.2 million.

Burlew himself was overwhelmed by the whole experience. He said he was totally unprepared for the response, and he struggled to keep up as his fund-raising skyrocketed. Right before he hit the launch button for his project, Burlew thought he might be making a terrible mistake, but it obviously wasn't.

As the drive grew, Burlew was always there to respond and give back. His caring, attention, and interaction made a huge difference. As one fan of Burlew's noted on an online message board, "He's the kind of guy who gets a million dollars and instead of buying a Lexus, immediately starts thinking how he can turn that into something for his fans that is WORTH a million bucks." When the fund-raising campaign ended, Burlew had support from 14,952 people.

Burlew also attributes his success to giving away the comic for free for years on the Web. He thought that giving away the material was a great way to market himself and gain recognition. His philosophy is that people are a lot more likely to spend money on things they know and that people want to own what they like, whether it be a DVD, CD, or book. And the fact that he was getting orders from fans meant that he shouldn't have any disappointed customers—they knew what they were getting into.

Other comic artist have also found profit through crowdfunding. Ted Rall, who describes himself as a comics journalist, is known for his political satire in independent newspapers. In 2010, he launched a fund-raising drive so he could travel to Afghanistan, and while staying there, he posted a regular comic on his Web site about events in that country. He raised $26,000 from 211 backers, and now his comics will be published in book form by Farrar, Straus & Giroux.

In the summer of 2012, a Web-based comic about video games called *Penny Arcade* launched a campaign to make its homepage advertising free for a year. The comic surpassed its goal of $250,000 by more than double, reaching $525,000. Having dedicated fans helped, and maybe their wacky incentives brought people in. For pledges of $1 to $14, Mike Krahulik (aka "Gabe"), a *Penny Arcade* creator, promised the wacky gift of shouting your name while chasing a duck.

MUSIC FOR THE MASSES

Bands and musicians who are trying to fund their recording projects have turned to Kickstarter in droves. As with most other projects, musical endeavors often succeed because the act has a large fan base. They may have

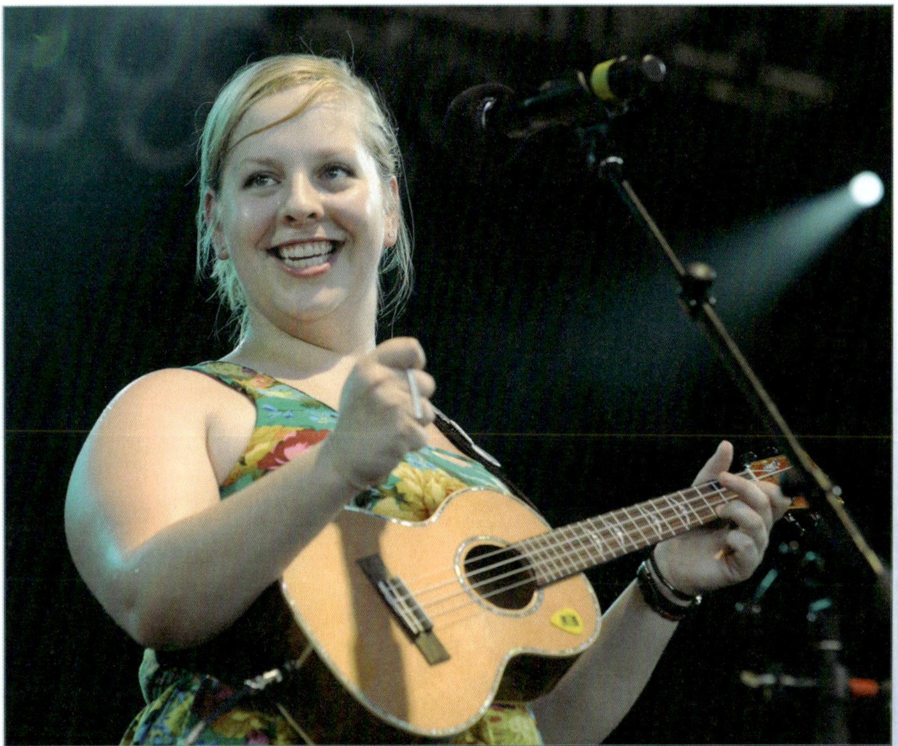

Julia Nunes became a success as a singer/songwriter after posting a homemade video on YouTube of her playing ukulele and singing. As her popularity exploded, she turned to Kickstarter to raise money to produce her third album.

developed the fans by posting a memorable video that has gotten hundreds of thousands of views, or they may have toured tirelessly around the country, gradually gaining fans as they played from one city to the next.

Julia Nunes launched a successful Kickstarter campaign by first creating a YouTube video that became hugely popular. From her bedroom in upstate New York,

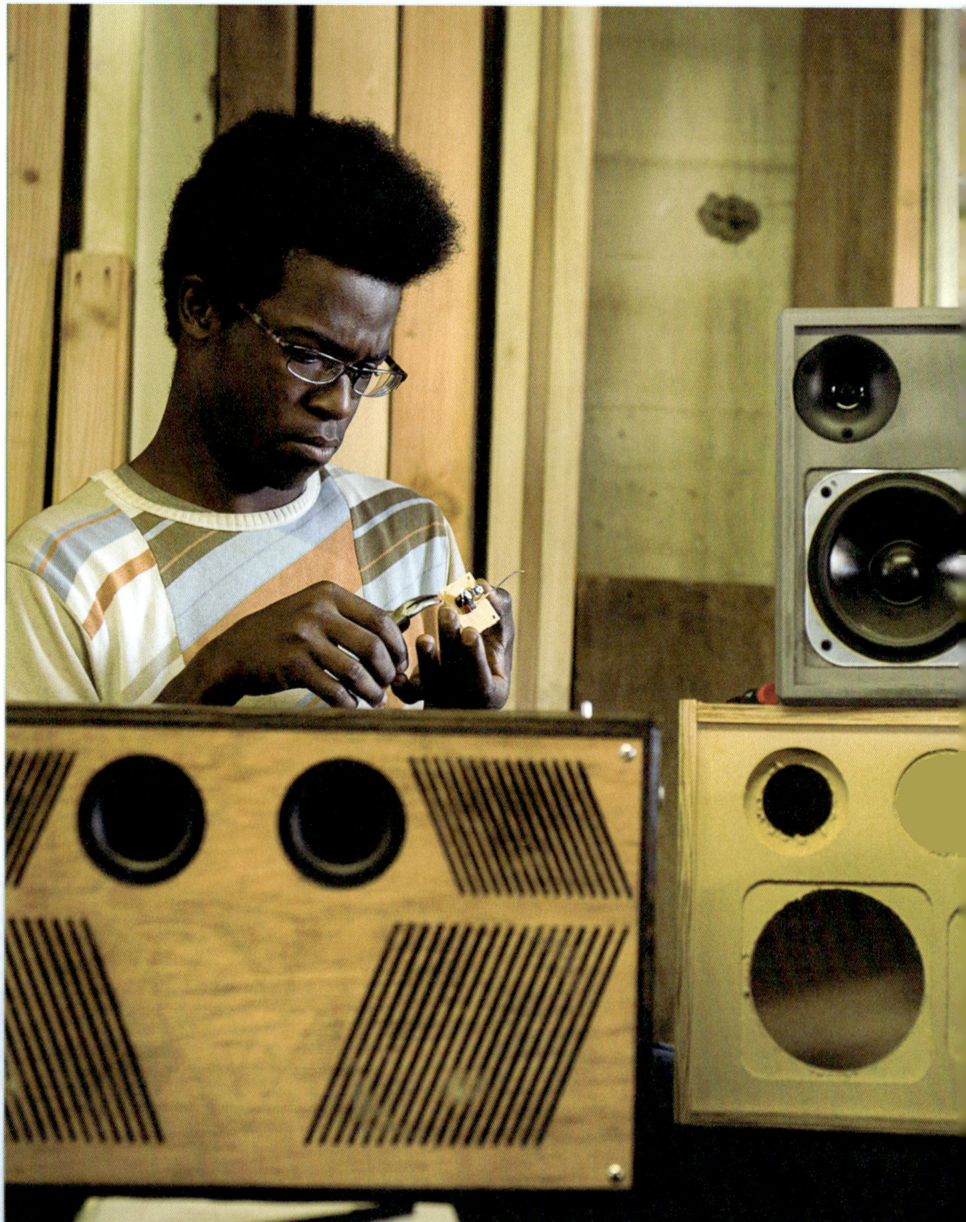

Michael Davis-Yates had a vision to create a unique boom box made of wood but with high quality sound, which he sought funding for on Kickstarter.

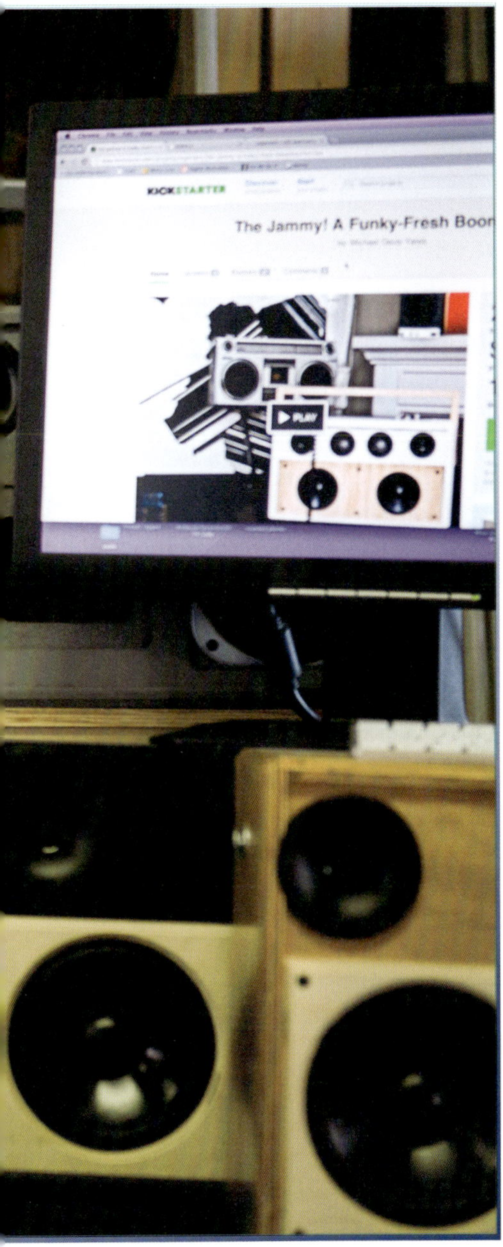

Nunes made a video of her singing a cover of the song "Build Me Up Buttercup" while she played ukulele. Her voice and performance were amazing, and the video takes a clever turn halfway through when a gang of her friends pop in out of nowhere to sing backup vocals.

The charming video gained her more than 2,000,000 views. From there, her musical career took off and she performed with the musical groups Ben Folds and Weezer. She even appeared on Conan O'Brien's talk show. After she recorded her first two CDs, she turned to Kickstarter and raised $77,888 dollars from 1,685 subscribers. The interesting point here is that a relatively small number of people made the difference for Nunes.

All Arts Can Benefit

Kickstarter's reach goes beyond music and film—artists, dancers, and writers have all been able to gain backing for their creative endeavors. Author, screenwriter, and blogger Chuck Wendig successfully used Kickstarter to write his young adult novel *Bait Dog*. Some of the art projects are more unique. Derek Tonks launched a Kickstarter project to build a full-size, fully wearable monster suit. Its creation would require twelve-inch (thirty-centimeter) custom stilts, mechanical hands with extended fingers, full body casting, and a facial mask fitted with animatronics that could be operated remotely. After a year of dedicated work and $3,620 of funding, Tonks created his "monster."

Chen, Strickler, and the team encourage offbeat projects like this because they believe that some artistic endeavors won't strike a chord with the masses but they deserve to be made and appreciated.

An article on Hyperbot.com described how a band called Lighthouse and the Whale had less than 2 percent of their fans donating to their recording via Kickstarter. When you look at Nunes's YouTube views compared to the number of people donating, it is a very small percentage of people actually chipping in. But still, that small percentage is making a big difference. A few high pledges really can fund a project.

FILMS FLOURISH

Kickstarter has been a champion of independent film production since its beginning. As of the start of 2012, about 4,500 films had been funded through Kickstarter. About $130 million had moved through the site, and about $45 million of that was for film projects.

Many Kickstarter-funded movies have gone on to see theatrical release. At the 2012 South by Southwest Film Festival in Austin, thirty-three films were funded through Kickstarter. Seventeen Kickstarter films went to the Sundance Film Festival in 2012. One of these films, *Black Rock*, was penned by the indie film actor and director Mark Duplass. The first feature-length documentary about China's infamous artist and activist Ai Weiwei, titled *Ai Weiwei: Never Sorry*, by Alison Klayman saw release at theaters throughout the country. Klayman's documentary received rave reviews in the *New York Times*, *Entertainment Weekly*, and *New York* magazine. John Kricfalusi, creator of *Ren and Stimpy*, successfully funded an animation project of his in 2012 called *Cans Without Labels*.

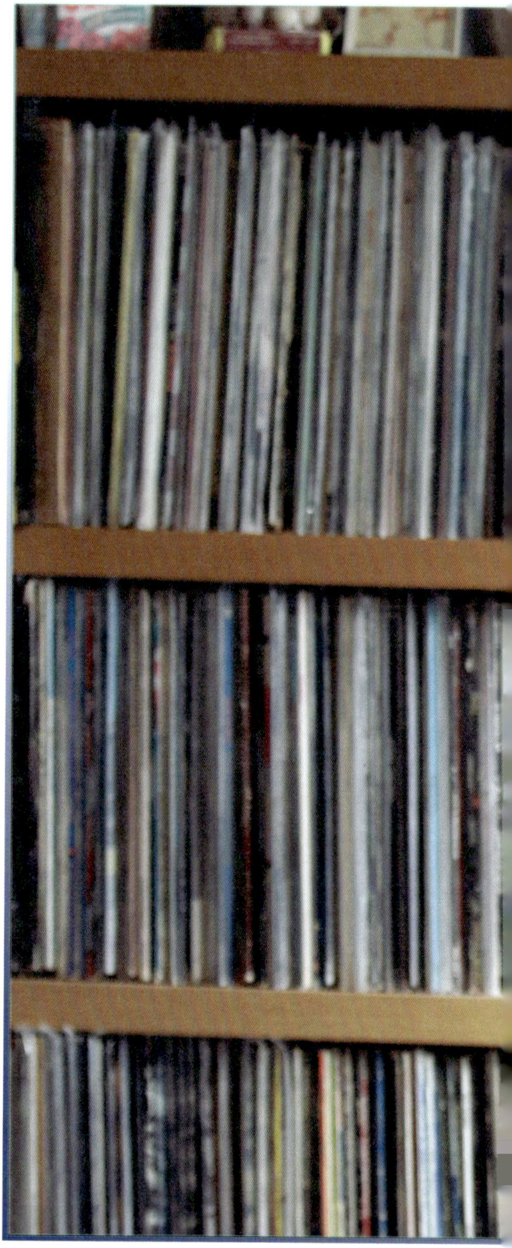

Vance Reeser is an up-and-coming animator who signed with Kickstarter early on in its history, in the fall of 2009. He was determined to raise enough money to produce his passion project, a short seven-minute animated film called *Lake Beast* about a man haunted by a strange glowing face he glimpses at the bottom of a polluted lake. He raised $2,025 from thirty-one backers.

Because of its success as a platform for raising money for independent films, Kickstarter has an official collaboration with Sundance Films. During its first year, Kickstarter received many inquiries from Sundance alumni. Strickler said that after a while it became clear that there would be an ongoing and steady stream of questions from these filmmakers.

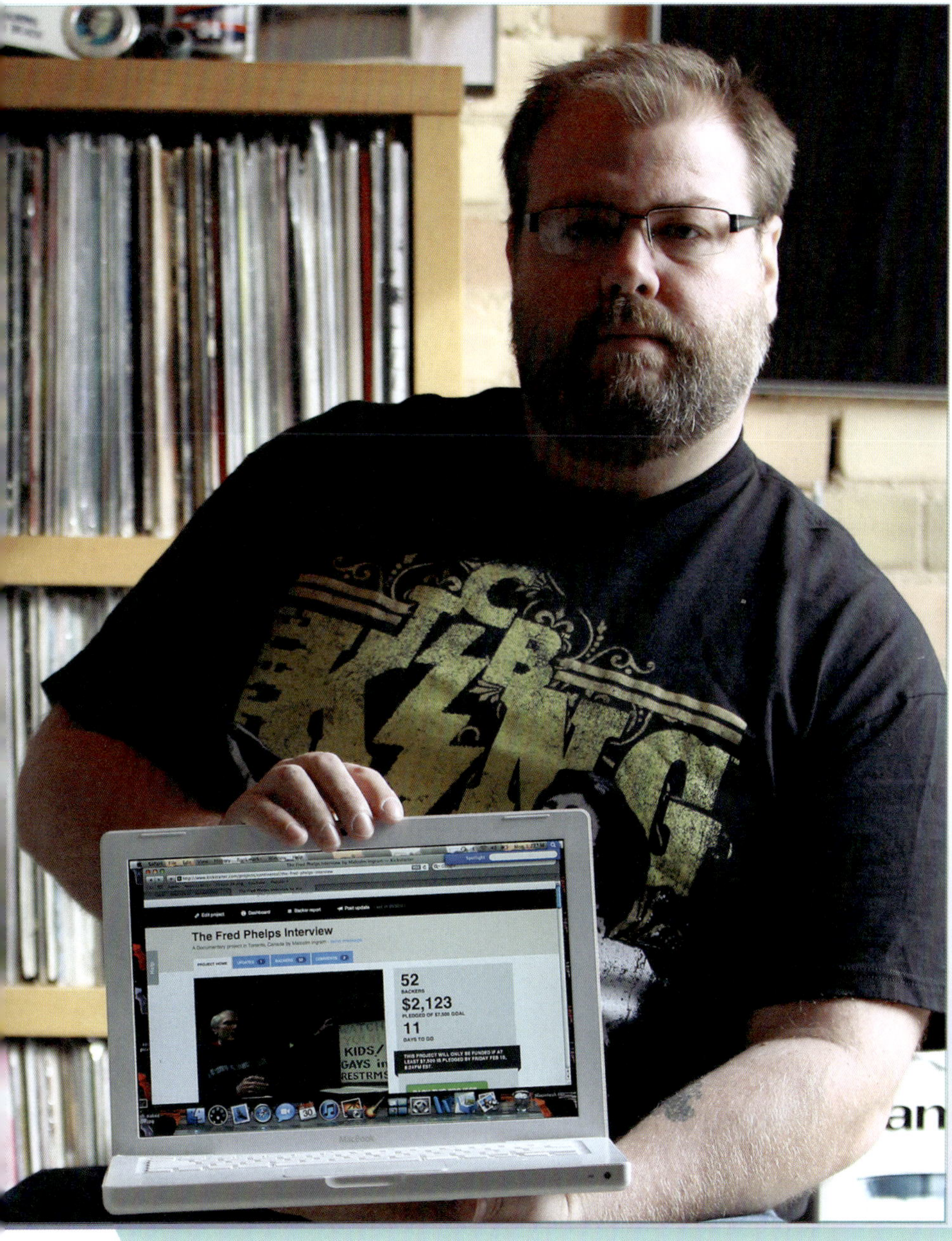

Documentary filmmaker Malcolm Ingram reached his goal and raised $21,865 through Kickstarter for his film project. Kickstarter has been very supportive of filmmakers.

Kickstarter began an official relationship and the organization became identified as part of Sundance Artists Services. The Labs is a summer program that is very selective and chooses a few composers, directors, and screenwriters to work with mentors such as Quentin Tarrantino.

Strickler has described independent filmmakers as "perma-fund-raisers" because they are always hustling and schmoozing with people who can help fund their motion pictures. The great part for artists is that those contributing to the films are not expecting a "return" on their investment. They are supporting the art they believe in for the art itself. There is no financial consideration. Strickler has said that most contributors don't expect something to be a massive hit; they are simply saying, with a donation, that they want this art to exist. Strickler said in an interview on Cinespect.com that this makes it possible for "quixotic and idiosyncratic" films to exist that are "purely art, with no notion of audience or market or any of those things."

As Kickstarter has grown, it has drawn in more established directors, in addition to little-known or unknown directors. Hal Hartley raised more than $56,433 for his independent film *Meanwhile*. Colin Hanks (son of Tom Hanks) is a fan of vinyl records, and raised $92,025 to produce his documentary on Tower Records. Many short films and Web series have been funded by Kickstarter as well.

SUPPORTING DOCUMENTARIES

As with Colin Hanks's documentary on Tower Records, many documentary films have been funded through Kickstarter. For some directors, the crowdfunding support has given them the lift they need to go to the next level. Jon Foy assembled a movie called *Resurrect Dead*. Focus Features picked up his film, and he won best documentary director at Sundance. Before this, Foy was cleaning houses, filming this project on nights and weekends over a course of about five years. Now Foy is a recognized filmmaker.

Two Kickstarter documentaries were short-listed in 2011 for the Best Documentary category of the Academy Award. One was *Battle for Brooklyn* about the Atlantic Yards project, which pitted local residents against real estate developers in a case of eminent domain, and *The Loving Story*, about the Supreme Court case that legalized interracial marriage.

In an interview with Documentary.org, one of the creators of *Battle for Brooklyn*, Michael Galinsky, said, "The vast majority of our supporters pledged at the $25 level, but we also had a number of $50, $100, and $500 pledges. I talked with a lot of people who told me that they were constantly watching the progress all day and thinking of other people to send the link to. As we suspected, they became invested in the process and became our essential allies in reaching our goal."

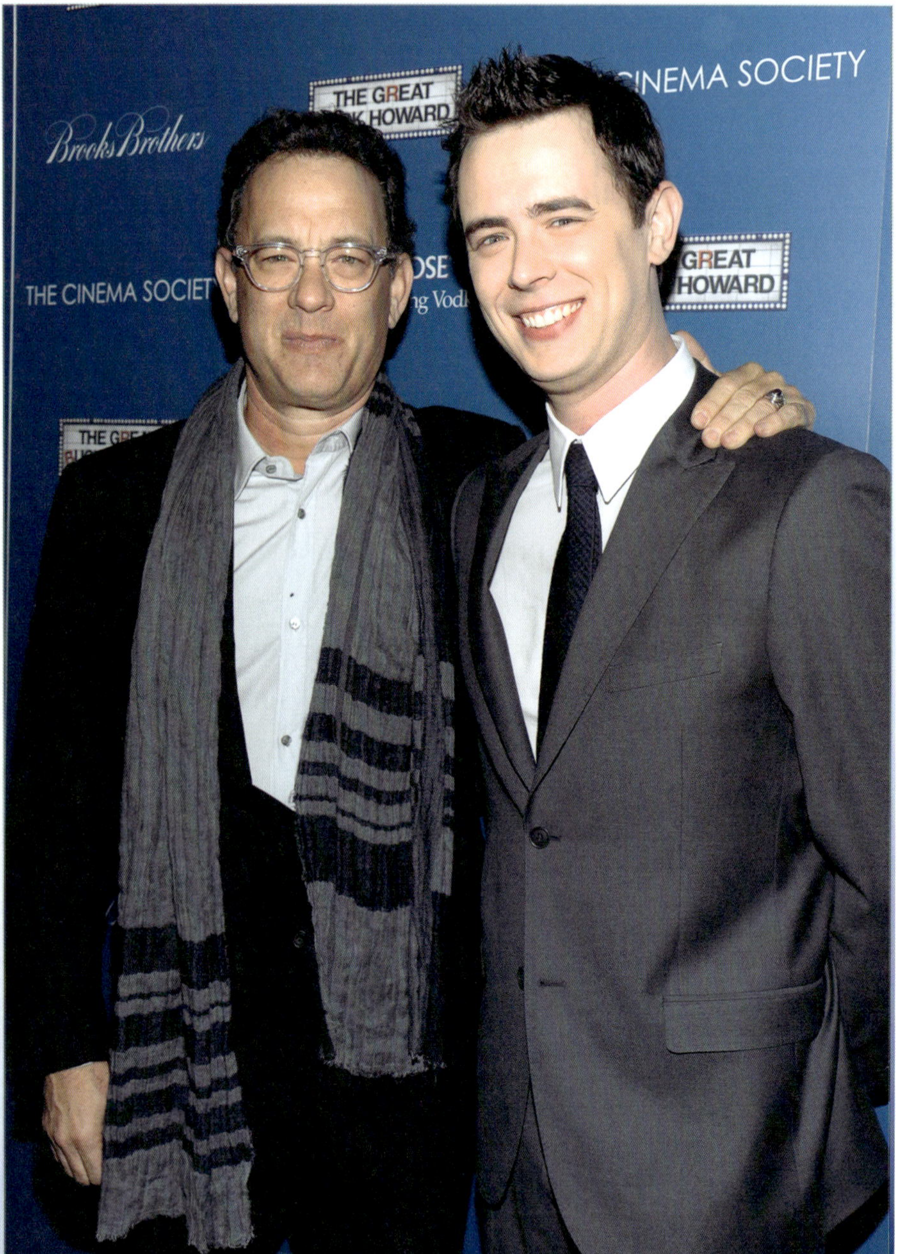

As more independent filmmakers successfully raised money through Kickstarter, established directors took notice. For example, Colin Hanks, the son of Tom Hanks, raised money for his documentary on Tower Records through the crowdfunding site.

Other documentaries that have raised money this way include ones about Devo, the game *Dungeons and Dragons*, the game *Minecraft*, and Bill Watterson's comic strip *Calvin and Hobbes*.

Many raise money to complete a project: Jennifer Fox had already filmed *My Reincarnation*, but she needed money for things such as music rights, postproduction, and subtitling services. In a world that seems more eager to embrace the blockbusters, films that challenge and explore real-world issues may be finding their audience through Kickstarter.

Chapter 4

Help for Innovators and Million-Dollar Ideas

Kickstarter has grown significantly via the world of unique gadgets and inventions. The story of the TikTok watchband is one of the site's most successful "inventions." The designer Scott Wilson came up with an idea for a watchband that would hold the iPod Nano. Scott has been very successful working for Nike, Microsoft, and Sony. Based in Chicago, Wilson now runs his own design studio called Minimal. When he first saw the Nano, he thought it would make a great wristwatch. Initially, he took his idea to manufacturers and to Apple itself, but they all rejected his idea. Apple thought it was too expensive to produce.

Wilson decided to produce the wristband himself and he set a modest goal to raise $15,000 on Kickstarter to get started. To drum up microsupporters, he offered those who contributed at least $25 one of his new wristband products. Basically, he was preselling his product. Wilson didn't expect the response he got. His drive far exceeded its initial goal, and he raised $941,718 with 13,500 backers from countries around the globe. At that point, it was the biggest Kickstarter success story to date.

With such success, guess who came knocking and wanted to sell the product? Apple, which had turned down the chance to produce the line, was now asking to distribute Wilson's creation. The basic wristband retails for about $35. Amazingly, Wilson's more upscale band called the LunaTik retails for about $80 and sold double the amount of the simpler version on the Kickstarter project.

Wilson said that he really gave the Nano a "home" and that there was nothing more gratifying than having all those supporters put money on their credit card for a product that didn't even exist yet. Amazingly, about three-quarters of those who donated didn't even own a Nano yet.

WATCHES COME BACK WITH A VENGEANCE

Oddly enough, one of Kickstarter's other huge success stories was also a wristband. Many people view the wristwatch as an outmoded, out-of-date piece of technology because most people can get the time off their mobile phone. A watch seemed like a product that would not generate much interest in this modern world. But in April 2012, a

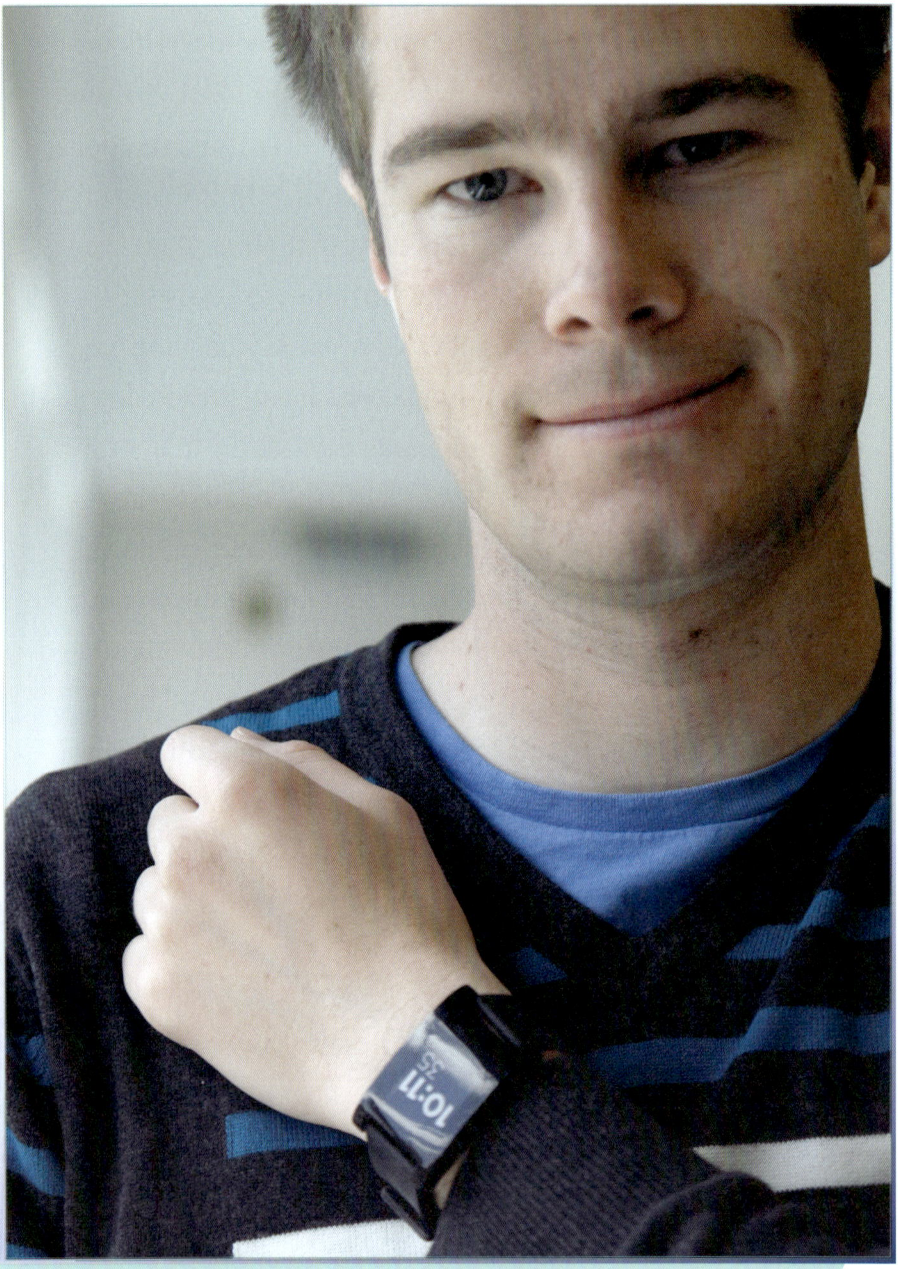

Inventors have found great success on Kickstarter, preselling many of their creations. Eric Migicovsky had one of the biggest hits in Kickstarter history, raising $10.3 million for his Pebble watch, featuring programmable watch faces.

three-person start-up called Pebble Technology set out to raise $100,000 to produce wristwatches that featured different programmable watch faces that link to the iPhone or Android devices.

Creator Eric Migicovsky has always been an avid cyclist, and he was looking for a way to access calls, texts, and e-mails without having to carry a phone with him. His idea for a watch that let you do this solved his dilemma.

The young founders of the company, all in their mid-twenties, first sought funding from venture capitalists and angel investors. They received some funding but not nearly enough. Migicovsky has said that he and his team weren't just looking to sell a product; they were looking to build a community.

Through Kickstarter, they basically presold their watches for $150 each. Their goal was far exceeded when they raised $10.3 million. Migicovsky said at one point the orders were pouring in at a rate of one every thirty-eight seconds. To fulfill the orders, he hired six people. It was great that the product was so popular, but it was also overwhelming. Kickstarter had reached a whole new level of potential.

In another example of popular funding, Casey Hopkins designed a solid-aluminum iPhone dock and went to Kickstarter to raise $75,000. He broke the $1 million barrier, raising $1.4 million. Kickstarter was no longer confined to raising money for art projects.

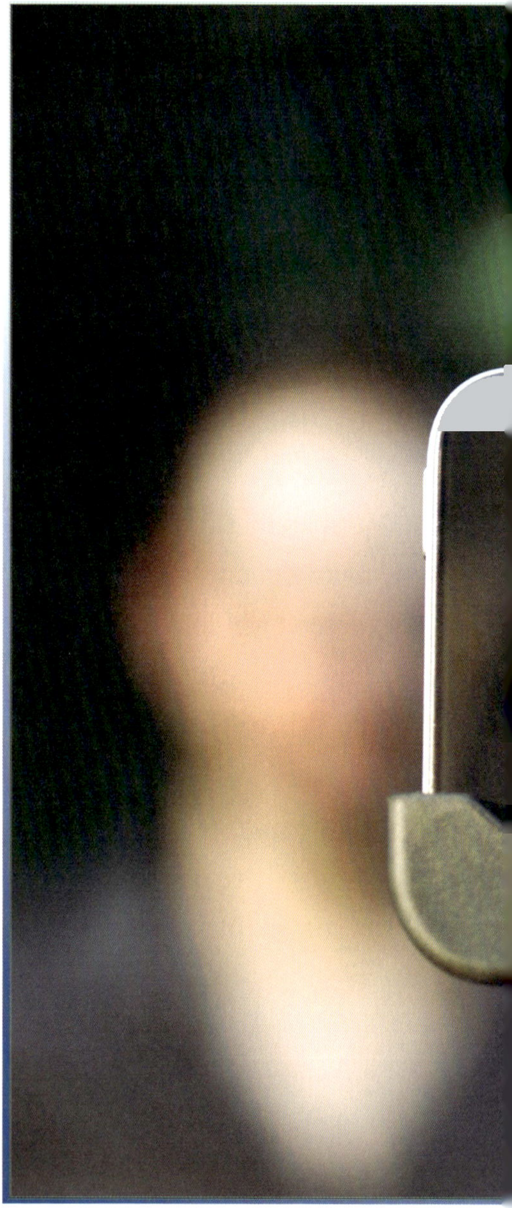

Obviously, innovators and entrepreneurs had seen the big potential of Kickstarter, and they were pushing the stakes higher. Ouya, a Los Angeles–based company, wanted to create a hackable, or modifiable, Android-based gaming console that would compete with PlayStation, Wii, and Xbox. It was an ambitious endeavor. In the summer of 2012, they set their target at $950,000. They raised $8.6 million and made promises to deliver the product by March 2013. Creators of a high-tech espresso machine that promised constant temperature and pressure to improve the quality of the drink sought $20,000 and got $369,000.

Some of the projects that have started out as one-time production models have developed into full-fledged

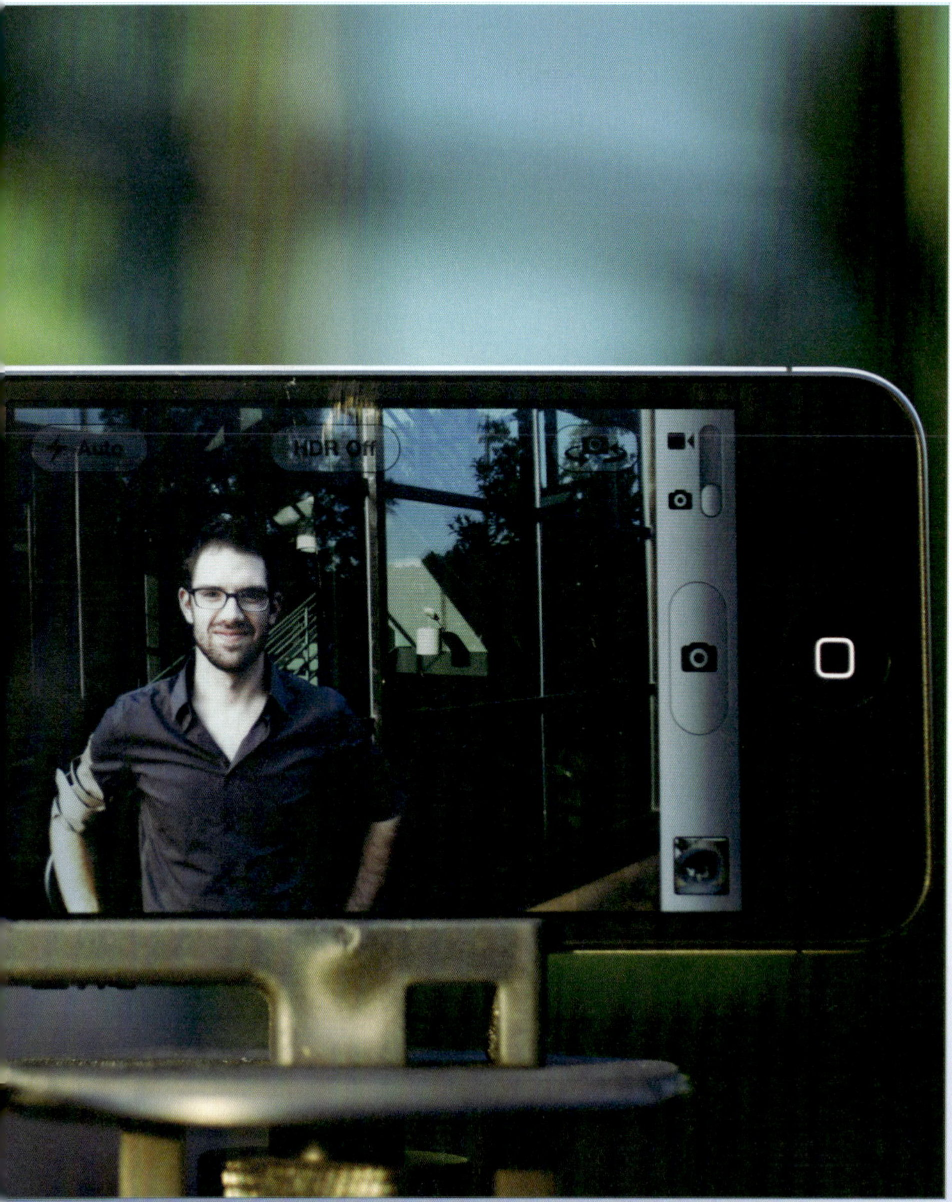

Tom Gerhardt *(pictured)* and Dan Provost raised more than $100,000 for a tripod that holds the iPhone 4, called the Glif. The business is doing so well that they quit their day jobs.

companies. ElevationLab in Portland, Oregon, is now manufacturing iPhone docking stations, and Touchfire, in Redmond, Washington, is producing a keyboard for the iPad. Tom Gerhardt and Dan Provost brainstormed an idea for a plastic tripod that would serve as a stand for the iPod 4. They called it the Glif and raised $137,000. Working with a factory in South Dakota, they manufacture the Glif and sell it online now for $20. Things are going so well, the pair have quit their day jobs as designers to work on the line full-time.

DEALING WITH SUCCESS

The founders of Kickstarter, however, may be a bit uncomfortable with Kickstarter's new role as a conduit to big commerce. They have always been more artistically inclined. Yancey Strickler has suggested in interviews that Kickstarter was not intended to be a tool for business-building and generating riches for entrepreneurs. On the site PurplePawn.com, Strickler said that in general they don't like their crowdfunding tool to be used as a way to start a business. But as entrepreneurial folks and small companies launch products through Kickstarter, the line can blur a bit. At what point is an operation too big to use the crowdfunding site?

Why don't budding entrepreneurs just set up a site and say they're selling pre-orders of a product? Many would say that somehow Kickstarter has captured a

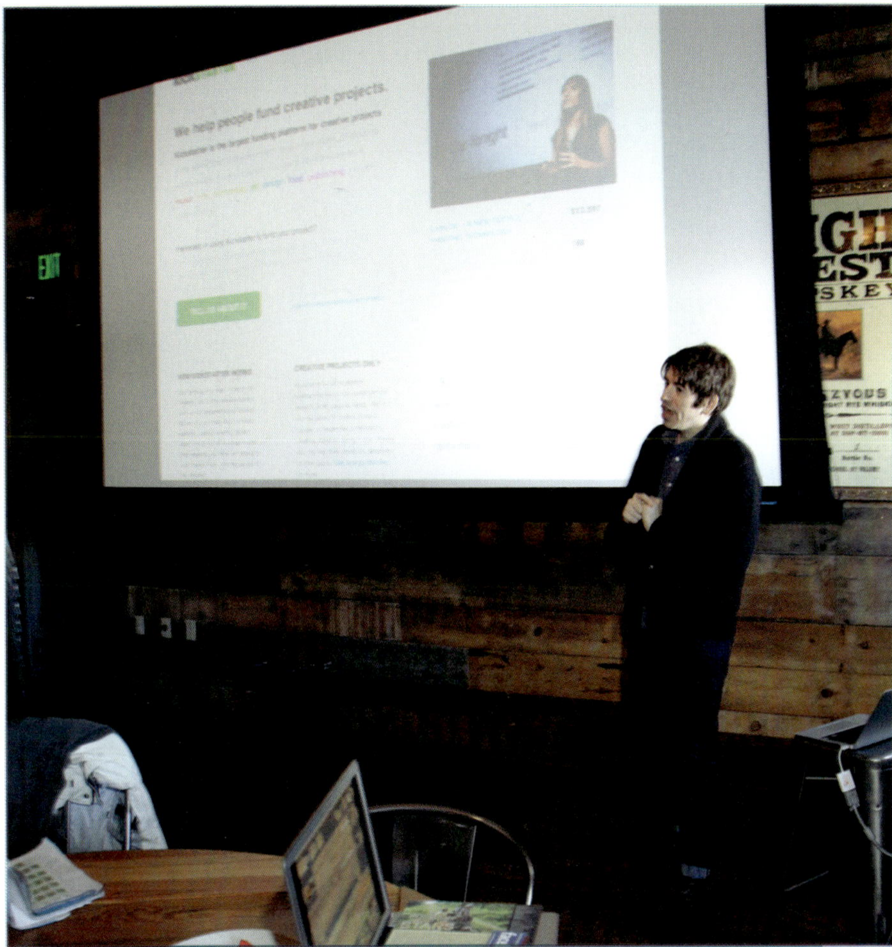

Yancey Strickler has said that so many people like Kickstarter projects because they're not just buying a product. They're becoming part of the story, the journey from inception to final completed project.

"feeling" or a connection with an audience. Strickler said that people are not just buying a product; they are buying an experience. Those who contribute are part of the product from inception to conception. They are part of

Tips for Having a Successful Kickstarter Project

Based on successful Kickstarter campaigns, here are some tips that can help people raise the money they need and then some.

Set the right amount. You want to raise enough to fund your project but not too much to scare people off. You might set your sights a little low but then write text that encourages contributors to give beyond the set amount and explain why that will help you. Justin and Jordan Coombs from Boulder, Colorado, raised $36,967 to develop their intergalactic role-playing game called *Star Command*. But they burned through the cash rapidly, paying for expenses they didn't figure in, such as lawyers to set up their business, music licensing fees, and promotional materials. The brothers took on more than $50,000 in debt to assure they will launch their product, but they may have set their fund-raising higher if they had more accurately estimated all their expenses.

Create a strong promotional video. People want to see that there are real people behind a project. A video can really help potential backers understand what they are contributing to, and if your video establishes a personal or emotional connection, this can be just the thing that drives people to help your cause.

Carefully consider your rewards. Think of what you're giving at each price level. Make sure you're not giving a perk that is more expensive or time consuming than the donation. Some people wind up spending much more time and expense on mailing and postage than they bargained for. Really look through what other people gave before as incentives. Kickstarter maintains the pages of all the projects, so you can go back and see exactly how other people ran their programs. Keith Knight, a comic book artist, successfully raised more than $40,000 for his campaign and he threw in some unique perks as the project progressed. Changing things up as you go along can motivate fans and others to jump in and contribute.

Communicate. Throughout your fund-raising, post updates on how your campaign is going and how your plans are going for getting the project set up.

Promote. Make sure everyone in the world knows about your campaign. Make a press release. Alert the media. Tell all friends, relatives, and neighbors. Ask folks you know to post an announcement about your campaign on their Web site or Facebook page—and of course, post it on your own Web site and Facebook page.

the journey. They feel more connected with the creators. And duplicating this type of environment could be difficult for anyone wanting to launch a business.

VIDEO AND COMPUTER GAMES

An area that crosses commerce and art is the world of computer games. The Ouya console has been a successfully funded game console, but video and computer games themselves have also been well-funded through Kickstarter.

Tim Schafer had worked for ten years at game maker LucasArts when he decided to form his own computer game design company in 2000 called Double Fine Production. Schafer's work leans toward slower, more thoughtful, yet more humorous, point-and-click games. He said that it can be hard to get funding for games like these when most of the world seems to prefer first-person shooters like *Call of Duty*. Schafer's games have dedicated fans, but they are not on the same scale as mega-hits such as *World of Warcraft*. *The Secret of Monkey Island* is a typical Schafer game. Players help a would-be pirate named Guybrush Threepwood make his way around an island overrun with pirates. Along the way, you click on various items you might use and solve puzzles. Fans of his work appreciate the humor and that his games are often very story driven. Many of the shoot-'em-up games have very little story. Other Schafer games are *Psychonauts* and *Full-Throttle*.

Schafer decided to take a 2012 project idea to the people. He set a goal of $400,000. That was a dollar amount that now seemed very reachable in the crowdfunding universe after quite a few people had raised that much or more via Kickstarter. Plus, for a video game budget, this was considered a very modest amount. Double Fine was the first major computer game studio to fund a project through Kickstarter, so Schafer hoped it would work. A unique part of the project, too, was that a documentary film crew would be following the Double Fine team throughout the entire process.

Donators came in at a swift rate. Just after eight hours of posting, it was fully funded. By the end of the day, Schafer had hit the $1 million mark. From February 8 to March 13, 2012, Double Fine raised an astronomical $3,336,372 with 87,142 backers.

Schafer has said that the process has been very rewarding because it takes the risk out of the process. Instead of sinking money into a game and hoping the audience will find it and buy it, here the audience had bought it in advance. Schafer said that he is always looking to break the traditional mold for funding and that the company may rely on crowdfunding for all future projects.

Schafer's success with Kickstarter motivated other game creators to crowdfund their projects. Jane Jensen, creator of *Gabriel Knight*, Al Lower, creator of *Leisure Suit Larry*, and Brian Fargo, who developed *Wasteland*,

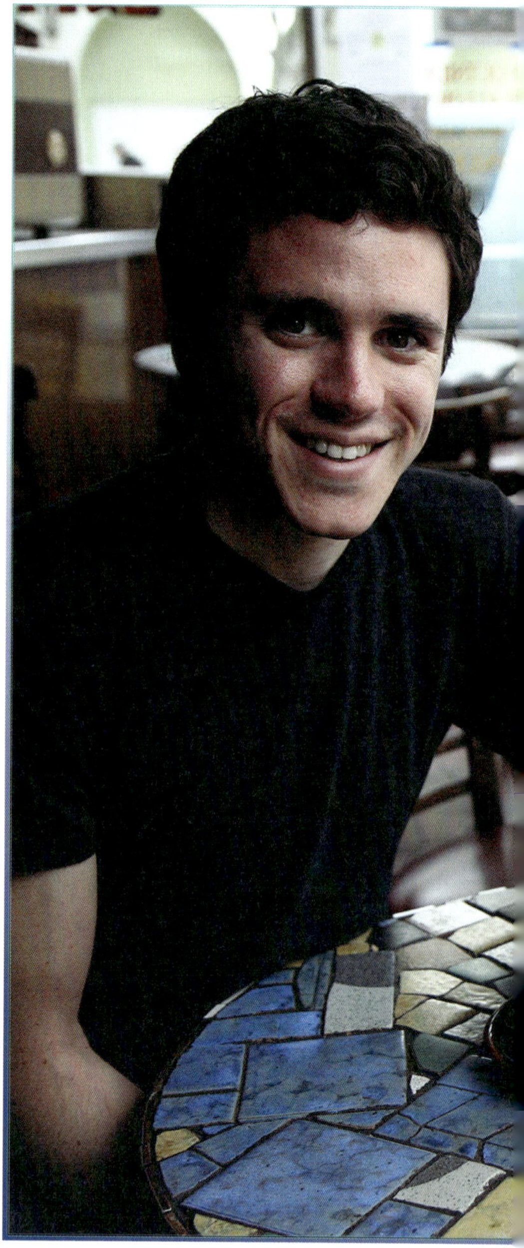

all used Kickstarter to raise funds. Fargo said he was so taken by the idea of crowdfunding that he wanted to do even more. So he launched a program called Kicking It Forward, whereby game developers who raised money via Kickstarter would vow to give 5 percent of their money raised to another Kickstarter project.

INNOVATIVE IDEAS COME TO LIFE

Some of the items that have been supported through Kickstarter have been truly different and innovative. Dave Jackson and Dave Petrillo, mechanical engineers from New Jersey, invented stainless steel capsules that are made to be put in a cup of coffee and keep it warmer for a longer period time.

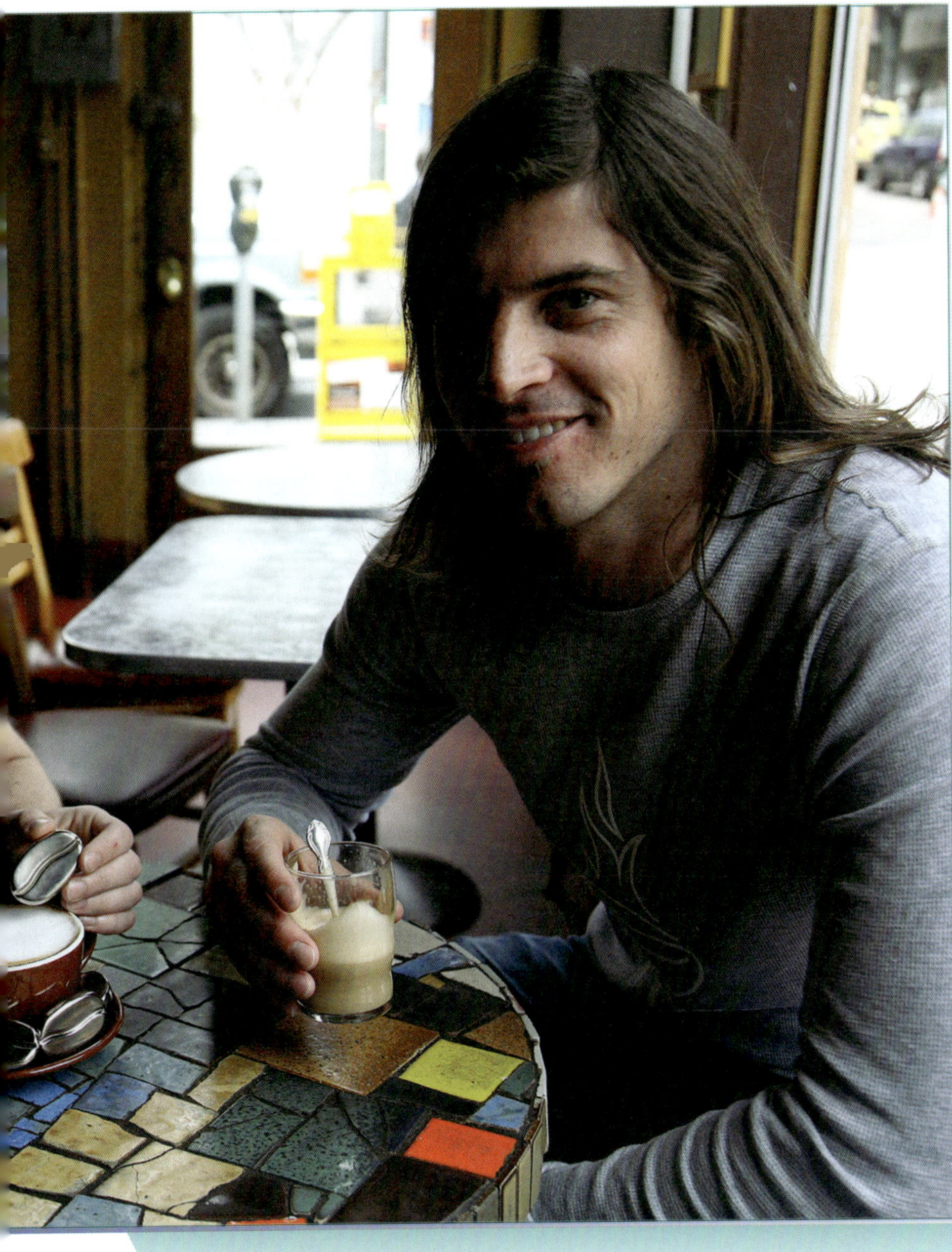

Kickstarter has always been home to truly innovative ideas. Dave Jackson and Dave Petrillo raised more than $300,000 for their steel capsules called Coffee Joulies, which keep coffee hot in the cup.

They named the product Coffee Joulies. They set a goal of $9,500 and raised $306,944. Australians Rob Ward and Chris Peters designed a sturdy iPhone case with a bottle opener at one end. They set a modest goal of $15,000 and raised $28,000.

When you start to look at projects focused on an invention, you can forget that not all projects are about making money. Two biologists funded their research of a little known species of bird called the Elegant Quail in Sinaloa, Mexico. Jennifer Calkins, who led the project, said on the Kickstarter Web site, "By contributing to this project you will support a study of this little known species as we examine its behavior and evolution in its natural habitat, a space encroached upon by both urban sprawl and tension surrounding narcotics trafficking."

Shawn Frayne and Alex Hornstein are building products based on microsolar panels and raising money to make solar pocket kits that people can use to charge cell phones and power small devices. A gadget called Twine connects to sensors in your home and then will send you a message wherever you are if the sensor is activated. For example, if a fire sensor goes off, Twine can send you a message. If you have a sensor in the basement warning you against flooding, Twine can send you a message. The drive raised $556,542 from an initial goal of $35,000.

Other projects have included an oil-spilling robot and a self-sustaining vehicle run on fuel made from algae.

Filabot grinds up recyclables such as milk jugs and soda bottles and then uses the resulting filament for 3-D printing projects.

Daniel Phillips funded a project to create gumball-style machines that would distribute seed bombs. Made from a mixture of clay, compost, and seeds, Phillips said that seed bombs are a means for combating the many forgotten gray spaces we encounter every day—from sidewalk cracks to vacant lots and parking medians. They can be thrown into urban sites to temporarily transform them into beautiful places.

There is a vast range of inventions and innovative ideas that people are thinking up, and Chen and Strickler are happy to be providing a format that is helping many of these concepts become reality.

Chapter 5

Growing Pains

As with many businesses that do very well, Kickstarter also has its share of people who do not like the service. About five out of ten Kickstarter projects fail. They do not reach their goal, and they do not get their funding. Of these 54 percent who do not reach their funding goal, there are many who are not fans of the Web site.

Bill Baird, for example, tried to raise $45,000 through the crowdfunding site to make a film called *The Origin of Sound*, about a trek to India. Baird was disappointed that the film only raised $2,233 and his team did not get to keep the funding. He has been vocal about his dissatisfaction with the service.

PROPOSALS THAT FLOP

But with Kickstarter, rejection can come even before a project is posted. The site turns down many proposals soon after they are submitted. Thousands have received this letter:

> Thank you for taking the time to share your idea. Unfortunately, this isn't the right fit for

> Kickstarter. We receive many project proposals daily and review them all with great care and appreciation. We see a wide variety of inspiring ideas, and while we value each one's uniqueness and creativity, Kickstarter is not the right platform for all of them. We wish you the best of luck as you continue to pursue your endeavor.

Chen and Strickler have said from the start that a project must be creative to be approved by Kickstarter. In the *Economist*, Chen said that the overwhelming majority of times, they reject a proposal because the creator has ignored the guidelines. Chen believes everybody should have a Kickstarter project because everyone has some kind of creative project that he or she thinks about.

Yet, go online, and you'll find many blogs where people are complaining that their creative projects were rejected. Some find that the acceptance policy is inconsistent.

One blogger complained that his wife dedicated weeks to developing a stuffed animal pattern that she wanted to get out to the world if they would support it. Kickstarter seemed like a natural fit, but they turned her down. Another site talked about how its idea to produce pillows with leopard skin prints was refused.

Even the acclaimed author Margaret Atwood has been rebuffed by Kickstarter. She presented her idea for

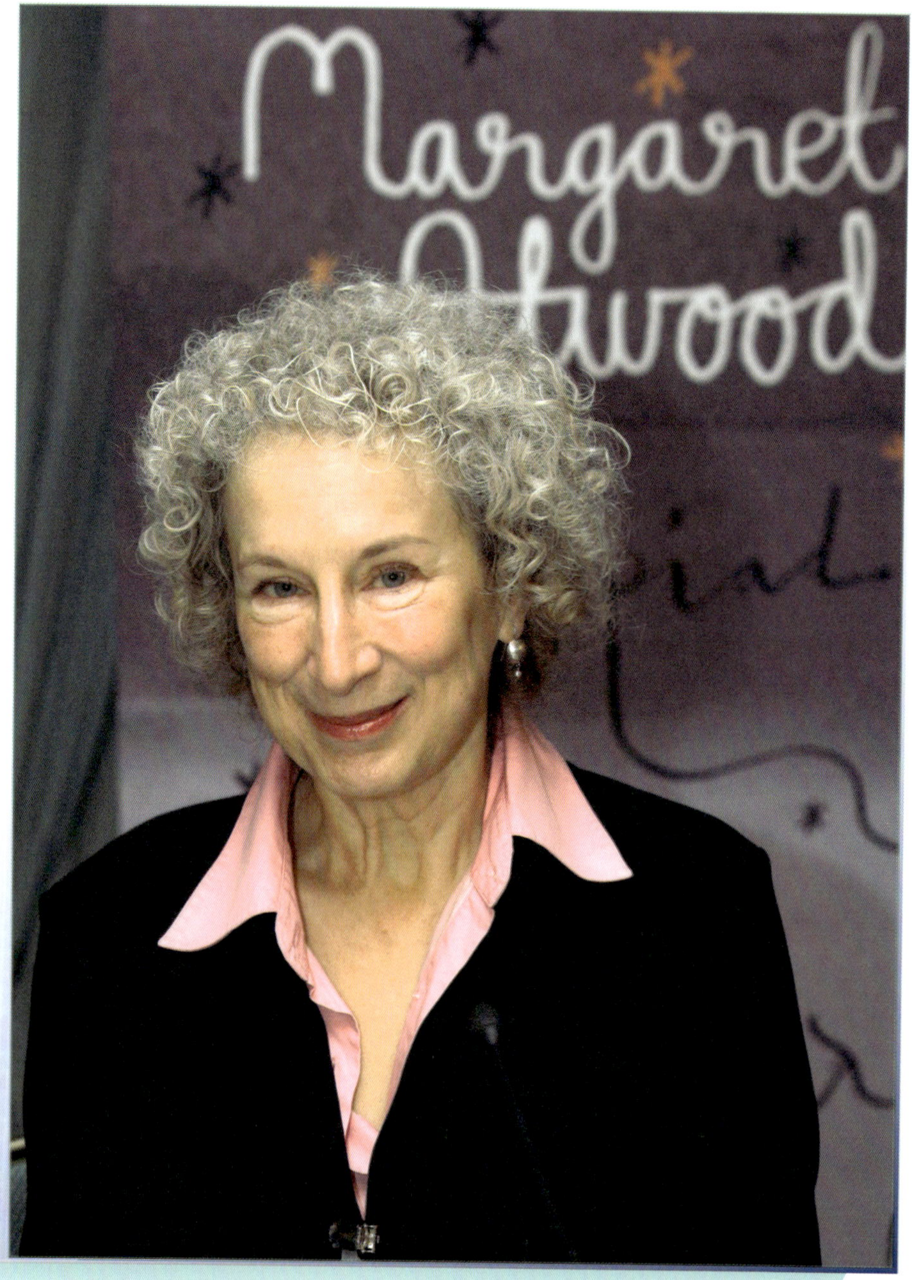

Has your idea been rejected by Kickstarter? Don't feel bad. Kickstarter has turned down many proposals, including one from acclaimed author Margaret Atwood.

a device dubbed Fanado that would provide electronic signatures to fans. Atwood said on Bookriot.com, "They told us we didn't meet their criteria. I still have no idea why." With a goal of $85,000, Atwood took the idea over to competitor Indiegogo and surpassed the funding goal, reaching $94,995.

At first, Kickstarter rejected a proposal from Synergy Aircraft. The company is creating an all-composite aircraft with a double-box tail. Designer John McGinnis has merged several unique drag-reduction technologies into a single package, and he hopes that the result is a modern, roomy, fuel-efficient, affordable family aircraft that will help spur a new era of innovation in personal aviation. Many fans of Synergy were upset about the rejection and sent e-mails and wrote blogs urging Kickstarter to reconsider.

This grassroots campaign appears to have given Kickstarter a change of heart, and they eventually approved the project. As of this writing, the company set a goal of $65,000 on the site to complete the engine and landing gear in the prototype.

As a result of the Synergy appeal, Kickstarter revised its guidelines. It now requires "additional information from design and technology projects so backers can make informed decisions about the projects they support. These requirements include detailed information about the creator's background and experience, a manufacturing plan (for hardware projects), and a functional prototype."

You still can't post any project related to charity, health care, or medicine or fitness-based projects. The team will also reject anything with obscene, hateful, or objectionable content.

Because Kickstarter does not accept projects related to health care or the medical field, health technology entrepreneur Alex Fair and founding Kickstarter product manager Mike Pence started MedStartr, which is basically Kickstarter for health care–related projects. It allows people to crowdfund medical start-ups. Fair was inspired by Kickstarter's rejection of his health technology ideas.

KICKSTARTER SCAMS

One of the questions that many contributors have is, "How do I know the person or group raising funds will go through with the project?" Or, "Will they send me or give me the incentive I was promised for contributing?"

Certainly, there is a great amount of trust involved. The primary "guarantee" that a project is real is the fact that most people contributing to a project are friends of the creator. Most creators do not want to rip off their friends. And most creators are genuine about their endeavors. If they don't fulfill their promise, they will generate great ill will and have little luck funding any future projects.

Still, some people may want to use Kickstarter to take the money and run. Little Monster Productions, "makers" of a gaming project titled *Mythic: The Story of Gods and Men*, canceled its crowdfunding pitch in May 2012 after backers began to question its legitimacy. One donator noticed that the art for the company's game proposal had been borrowed from several other game designers. Another donator searched the company name online and found that Little Monster Productions did not exist except for the Kickstarter project. Another person noted that there was no way to contact the company on its Web site, and the photos of its "office" were lifted from another Web site. Little Monster Productions responded to skeptics online saying that game development was underway, but it couldn't really defend itself, and the project was taken down.

The fact that a scam made it this far sounded alarm bells for those who have been supporting crowdfunding. One critic wrote on the Kickstarter comment page, "What worried me the most is how Kickstarter allowed this [the Mythic project] to be posted in the first place. A simple Google search, and I found out for myself this was very shady."

RISK IS PART OF THE PROCESS

Besides a pitch being an out-and-out scam, some projects may never get made and some creators may not fulfill the incentives they promised. Chen and Strickler say that those who donate understand the gamble. Even if the product does get made, there is no accounting for how

The JOBS Act and Crowdfunding

By showing how effective crowdfunding can be, Kickstarter was the inspiration for part of a U.S. government bill that will allow crowdfunding as a foundation for helping small businesses. Portions of the Jumpstart Our Business Startups (JOBS) Act lets start-ups raise seed capital from any number of investors in small amounts through crowdfunding platforms.

Kickstarter does not plan to enter this arena yet. Kickstarter is in the business of funding projects with definite end dates, not selling shares. Yet, sites such as Launcht in the United States and Crowdcube in England will guide start-ups through the process. This will give potential investors the opportunity to support new ventures by buying shares in the companies. Participants can raise as much as $1 million a year without having to do an initial public offering (IPO), a step requiring state-by-state registrations that can cost a lot of money.

Critics, though, are cautious that this new allowance for investing will be too unregulated and possibly lead to scams. They also fear that small investors could lose funds on risky ventures. Groups such as the North American

Securities Administrators Association said the bill would promote the fleecing of unsavvy investors. Proponents of allowing people to make investments through crowdfunding think that it will help spur the economy and create jobs.

the money is spent. Donors don't get to see how every dime is used. They just have to trust that it is being well spent.

Kickstarter has had to respond to angry backers who were promised a product in return for their donation but never received it. For example, Hanfree iPad accessory, Eyez HD video recording glasses, and Juicies colorful cables for iPods, iPads, and iPhones all raised more than $400,000 together in May through July of 2011, but donors have been notifying Kickstarter that they never received promised incentives.

Kickstarter issued an official response: "It's in the backers' hands to exert collective pressure. It's a creator's job to complete their project, satisfy backers, or refund backers' pledges." Competitor Indiegogo has recognized that crowdfunders may experience problems with projects, and they have set up a "24-hour-a day customer happiness team" ready to take calls and deal with customer concerns. Kickstarter will go after outright frauds, but in many cases, it's hard to determine if a project tried and just could not succeed.

Many of those who contributed to the Hanfree iPad accessory fully expected to receive products from the company, but the founder of the business basically told supporters that he had run through the money and there would simply be no product. One Arizona lawyer who contributed $70 intends to sue.

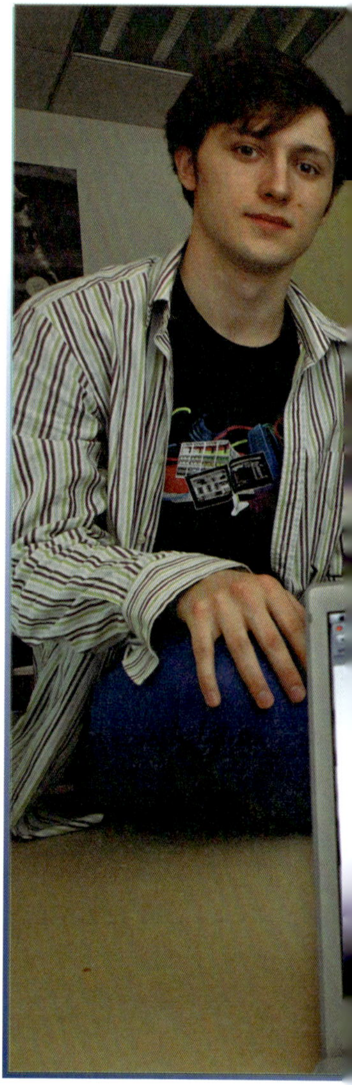

The North American Securities Administrators Association (NASAA) has warned that crowdfunding is growing and that consumers should be aware of more and more scams. In August 2012, the Massachusetts Securities Division charged a Lowell, Massachusetts, man with a crowdfunding scam that bilked twenty investors, who thought they were investing money in a gaming site, out of $153,396.

DARK SIDE OF THE BOOM

As they were about to graduate from New York University, four students posted a project on Kickstarter called Diaspora. Their plan was to build a Web site that would be an open-source social network that would also protect all of one's private information. The site would give users ownership of their information. Maxwell Salzburg, Daniel Grippi, Raphael Sofaer, and Ilya Zhitomirskiy set a goal to raise $10,000 via crowdfunding to start their new Web site. Although

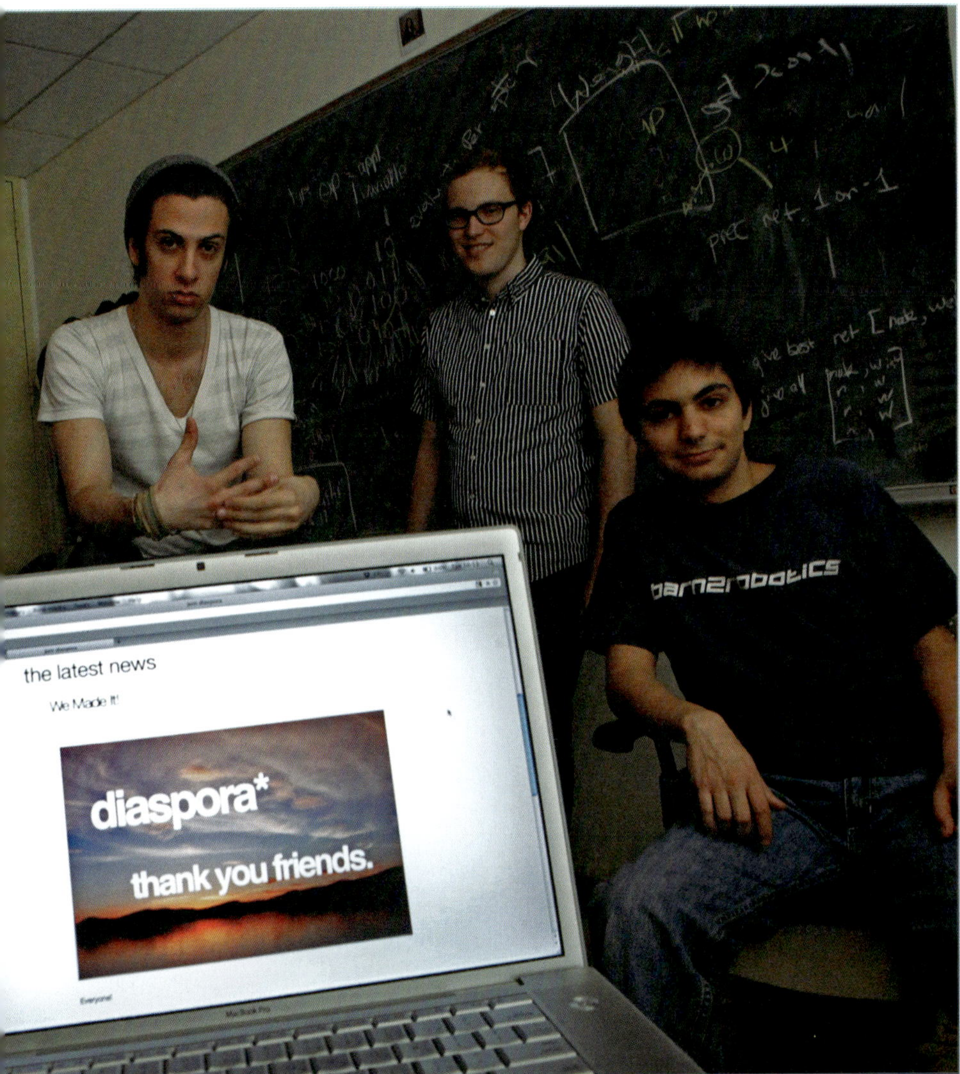

New York University students Ilya Zhitomirskiy, Daniel Grippi, Maxwell Salzberg, and Raphael Sofaer started a social networking site call Diaspora (www .joindiaspora.com) with funding from Kickstarter. Ilya, allegedly overstressed with starting the new business, committed suicide at age twenty-two.

their pitch video on Kickstarter was far from professional, the project captured the attention of the media. They were seen as possible competitors of Facebook. This idea that a small start-up could possibly compete with the massive social network appealed to many people who were dissatisfied with Facebook's services. Also, Facebook had been receiving mounting criticism regarding its privacy policies when it came to user information. By the end of their drive, the Diaspora group had generated $200,641.

About a year from its 2010 Kickstarter launch, the Diaspora team had built a social networking site similar to Facebook where users owned their data. About six hundred thousand

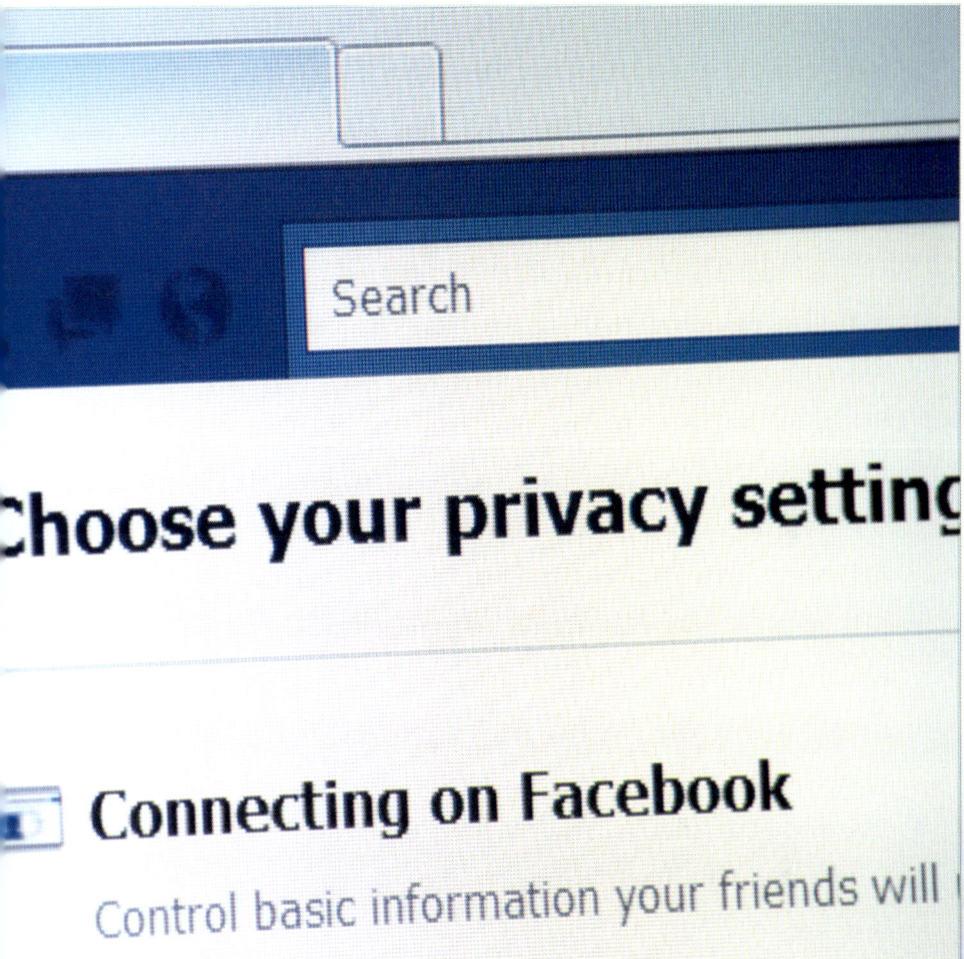

Many Kickstarter supporters liked Diaspora because it offered an attractive alternative to the strict privacy policy of Facebook. Diaspora, however, is still struggling to gain users.

people were using the site, but it was not the general population, and users weren't spending much time on the site. In the meantime, Google released GooglePlus, and it had a social networking aspect that looked a lot like Diaspora. Diaspora was struggling to attract users.

By the fall of 2011, the stress seemed to have gotten to founding member Ilya Zhitomirskiy, and he committed suicide. The team was devastated and questioned its whole decision to become involved in the business. Zhitomirskiy's mother said that if he had stayed in school and not followed this path, he probably would have been alive today. After some soul searching, the rest of the team eventually regrouped and is forging ahead. However, skeptics wonder as Diaspora lurches forward if it can be the site it set out to be. Others question if getting a huge amount of financial backing and attention is healthy for a start-up—especially for young people who have no experience in starting a business.

TAKING THEIR SHARE

Another part of the Kickstarter system that bothers some users is the fact that Kickstarter takes 5 percent of every program that is fully funded. Further, 3 to 5 percent of each targeted amount reached goes to Amazon Payments, which processes the transactions.

Some people connect their PayPal accounts to Amazon to make donations easier. While you must have a U.S. bank account to conduct business on Kickstarter, that could change.

COMPETITORS CROWD IN

With the success of Kickstarter, competition is inevitable. And many of these competitors are trying to encourage business in the areas Kickstarter does not support. A site such as Indiegogo lets users fund any sort of project—it could be for a trip, an operation, or a charity. Other sites zero in on a very specific niche such as medicine or journalism. Many don't use the all-or-nothing financing policy of Kickstarter, and some take smaller fees.

Indiegogo may be the biggest competitor for Kickstarter. Indiegogo hosts projects from around the globe. The company charges 9 percent on every dollar raised, which is higher than Kickstarter, but there is no processing fee for Amazon, so charges are comparable. But if you reach your fund-raising goal through Indiegogo, you pay only 4 percent. Indiegogo seems to have very few restrictions as far as content for the fund-raising. One recent drive was for a memorial fund for a man who was struck by a car and killed, leaving behind his wife and son. Another drive is helping to support a jaguar rescue mission at a zoo in Belize. Indiegogo also boasts partnerships with businesses, such as MTV and VH1, which may help increase exposure for artists who participate on the site.

RocketHub is similar to Kickstarter, with an all-or-nothing funding platform. The difference is in payment. RocketHub charges your credit card or withdraws PayPal funds immediately.

Crowdtilt bills itself as a group-funding site. The angle is that projects are started by a few people who are coming together to raise money for a plan.

There are a lot of sites facilitating crowdfunding, especially directed at start-up businesses—WeFunder, Startup Addict, and

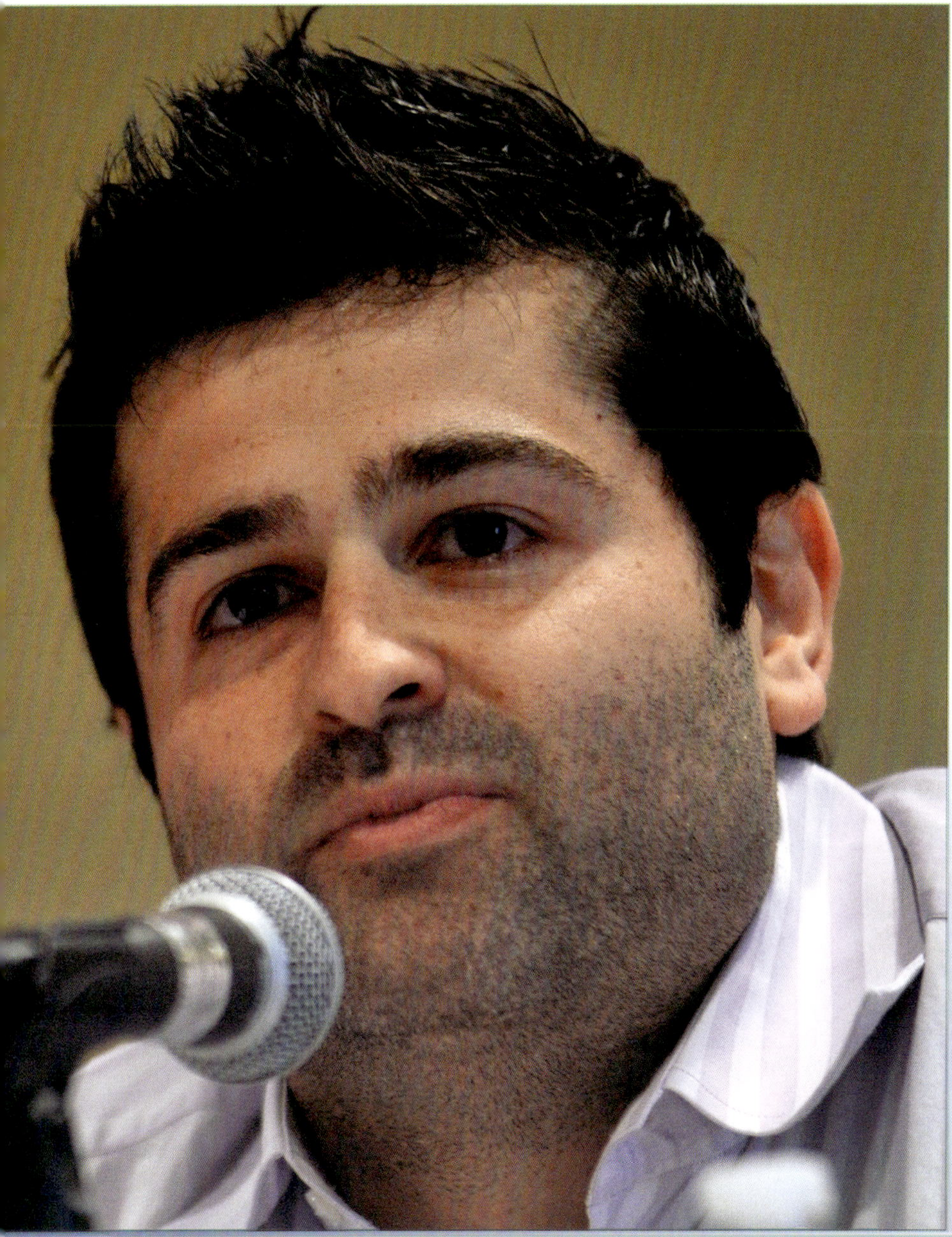

Kickstarter now has several competitors. Slava Rubin *(pictured)* is the cofounder of IndieGogo, a crowdfunding site that accepts all types of projects and lets creators keep money pledged even if the funding goal is not met.

Believers fund new business ideas. Quirky is aimed specifically at product designers and inventors who want to launch an original item.

Sellaband deals exclusively with music projects and takes 15 percent if the artist reaches the targeted amount. Sellaband takes a bigger cut than Kickstarter, but it focuses strictly on music from around the globe.

With the incredible success of Kickstarter, you can expect to see the launching of more sites that are based on this crowdfunding concept. Whether any can reach the height of Kickstarter remains to be seen.

Chapter 6

What's Next for Kickstarter and Crowdfunding?

In the spring of 2012, Kickstarter celebrated its third birthday. The company had grown tremendously in a very short amount of time. More than a million backers had chipped in $274 million to more than twenty-eight thousand projects.

In an interview with *Wired* magazine, Strickler said that he and Chen still like the more idiosyncratic projects that might not be big moneymakers. They have always pushed the idea that their crowdfunding site is the place to go for projects that might not make money in the real marketplace. However, recent history has shown that Kickstarter is the place to raise capital in excess of a million dollars.

Strickler has admitted that much of the site's big revenue has been coming in from products that are not yet made at the time of funding, and the Kickstarter team is looking at what this growing trend means. Is there a danger of Kickstarter being seen as a site for preordering products rather than raising funds for more artistic ventures? Could Kickstarter turn into an online catalog where customers are buying gadgets and games in advance? Could it lose its appeal as a Web site that supports homespun creativity and become a capital-raising tool that seems more about big business than helping the small businesses?

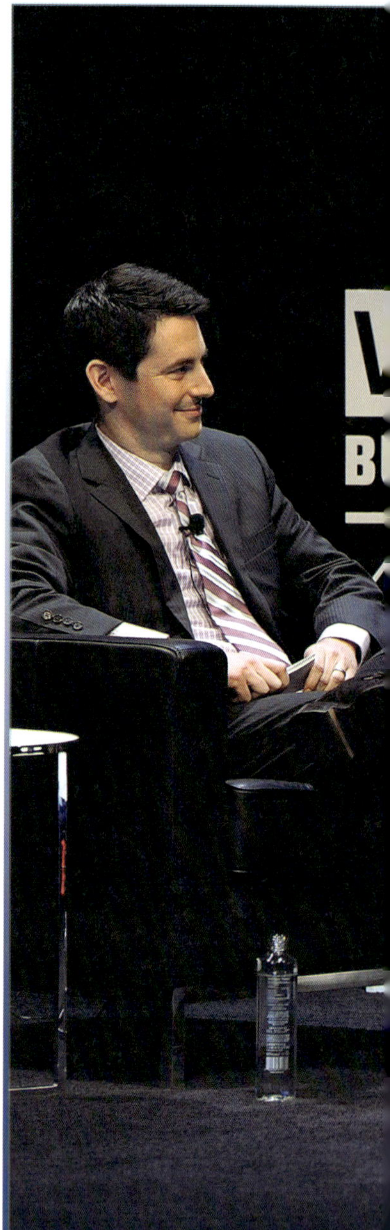

Despite these concerns, Kickstarter shows no signs of slowing down. With campaigns topping a million dollars, more and more business-minded people are turning to Kickstarter as a serious option to raise capital.

CAN A PROFESSIONAL PITCH BACKFIRE?

Strickler and Chen stress that the foundation of Kickstarter is still about the homespun idea. It is about helping people without resources to carry out their creative dream. But some

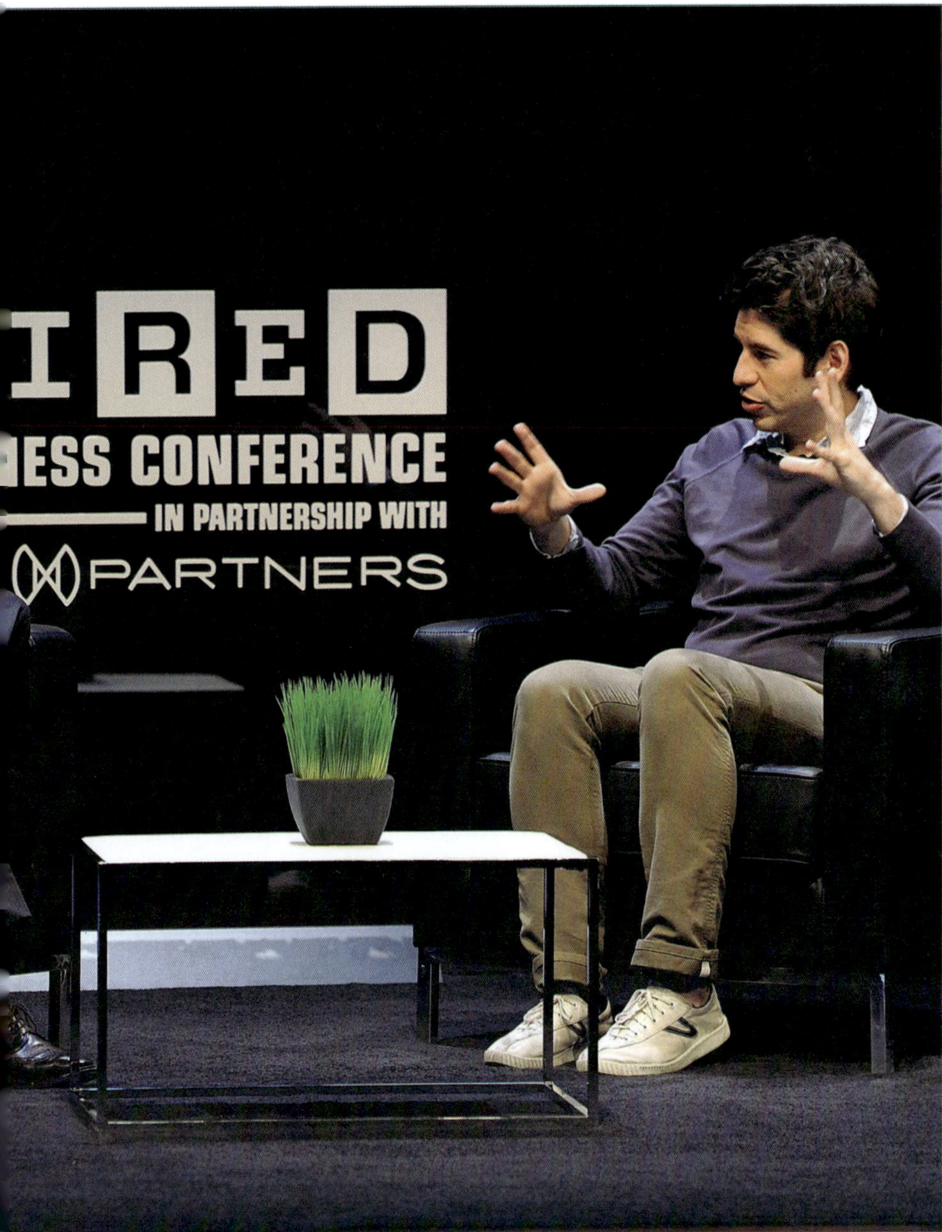

Kickstarter has had explosive growth in a few short years. In an interview with *Wired* magazine, Strickler recognized that the site has helped some very commercial products, but he emphasized that Kickstarter is dedicated to creative projects above all.

fund-raisers may be losing sight of this. They may appear too slick, professional, and corporate in their pitches.

In early 2012, seasoned video game producers Alexei Tylevich and Ryan Payton set out to raise money for a game called *République*. After the Double Fine game project brought in $3.33 million, Payton set their target at $500,000, thinking that was achievable. Basically, they needed ten thousand people to preorder their game.

They launched their product with a video that was polished and professional, assuming this would show that they had the resources to carry out their ambitious plan. They had invested a lot of time and money in the video, with cutting-edge sophisticated sound, editing, and images.

A week into their campaign, visitors were checking out the game, but they weren't pledging in the numbers that Payton expected. Instead, visitors were posting comments basically indicating that the game was so well-produced that the creators appeared not to need the money.

Payton was frustrated by the reaction, but he understood. As he wrote online on the game news site Gamasutra.com, "I was standing on a street corner in a freshly pressed suit holding an iPad with a typed out message 'Need money.'" If it looks like you already have a lot of money, people are far less likely to give you money. The crowdfunding site had always been dedicated to helping the guy without the resources to succeed, so you couldn't post a plan looking like you already had big bucks.

Payton also had an "LTTP" theory as to why the funds were not flowing in. LTTP is his shorthand for "late to the party," and Payton felt that users were cooling on Kickstarter. He noticed that gamers were complaining about the frequent coverage of crowdfunded game projects. There was a sense of overload when it came to crowdfunding. It almost seemed like everyone had their hand out and was looking for money.

Payton zeroed in on the incentives that they would give to donors. A fictional book companion and collector's edition of the game turned out to be big motivators for people to take out their credit cards. His first pitch video played down the people behind the project, so he switched gears and started posting videos on Kickstarter emphasizing the team behind the product. Payton found that the human element paid off and got a much better reaction. They also did a heavy public relations campaign to notify the world of their game.

Eventually, these seasoned game producers found their audience and received support from the gaming community. Yet, getting to the finish line was nerve-racking. The day before the deadline, *République* had $335,000 in pledges—far from its $500,000 goal. Articles had appeared online saying that they might miss their goal. In the last twenty-four hours of their campaign, Payton and his team posted a new video and hosted a party posted on the streaming video site Livestream.com as a thank-you to the more than seven thousand people who had pledged. The final twenty-four hours were an amazing blur to Payton. Pledges were coming in at a rate of about $1,000 per minute. The team surpassed its goal, raising $555,662 with 11,611 supporters chipping in.

SOMETIMES A SLOW PACE

Strickler has been warning Kickstarter supporters that making the products takes time, and some supporters can get frustrated. A survey published in July 2012 by Ethan Mollick, a professor at the University of Pennsylvania's Wharton School, found that 75 percent of technology and design-related projects on Kickstarter did not finish on time.

There is growing concern that more creators will not complete their project or they will not deliver their promised gifts for the donations given. OpenVizsla is one of the campaigns that became known for its inability to deliver. Two developers who went by Pytey and Bushing raised over $80,000 to build a device that could connect to a computer, take its data, and crack open its operating system. Two years later, the company had not delivered on its promise—the partners said they underestimated the expense. Several supporters of this project expressed their

A Formula for Success

When looking back at the data over the first three years of its history, it's interesting to see what works best. Successful projects have averaged thirty-eight days, while failed projects average forty-three days. Successful projects have an average target goal of $5,487 versus $16,365 for projects that have failed. The percentage of funded projects that have received more than double their goal is 8.5.

disappointment at the failure and said that Kickstarter needed to have some level of accountability.

However, the Kickstarter team believes that the crowdfunding community needs to police itself. Users need to alert others to scams and warn each other of the risks involved in participating in crowdfunding programs. The bottom line is that crowdfunding will always have an element of risk, and donors have to accept that fact.

STAYING TRUE TO THEIR CREATIVE MISSION

Strickler plans to keep the site going down the same path of supporting creative projects—even if they are not destined to make a million dollars. If you go to the

Kickstarter Web site, you can see that he favors the truly unique and innovative.

Right now the categories Kickstarter funds are art, comics, dance, design, fashion, films and video, food, games, music, photography, publishing, technology, and theater. One would expect that the team may expand the categories, as long as they are creative.

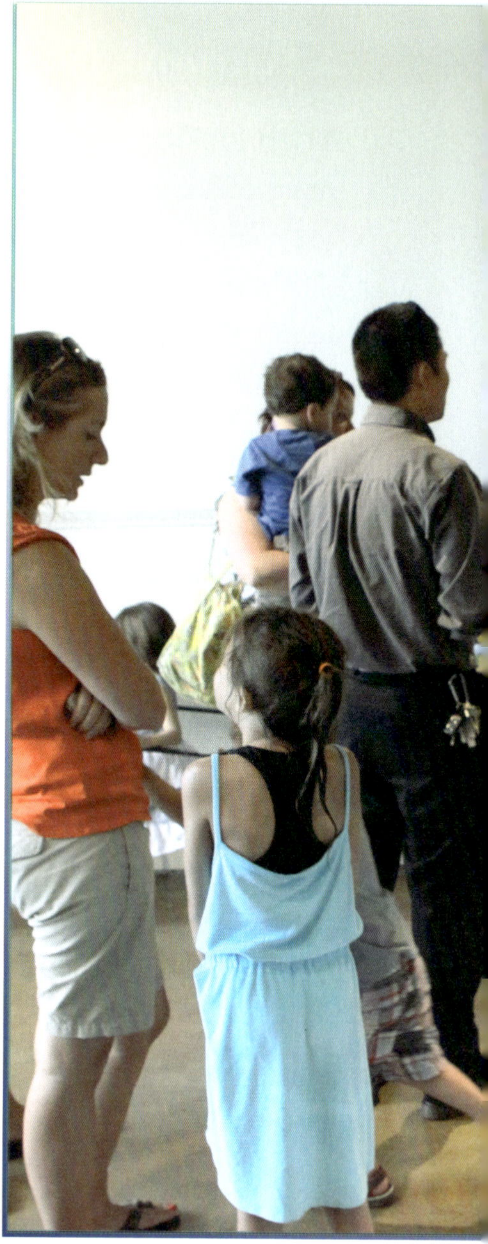

In the spring of 2012, Chen said that the team is looking to expand into urban design with projects such as innovative bike lane designs, bike racks, and community gardens. Chen said they're looking at exactly how these plans would fit into the Kickstarter structure. In an interview on the Web site GigaOm, Chen said that they're investigating science as a category.

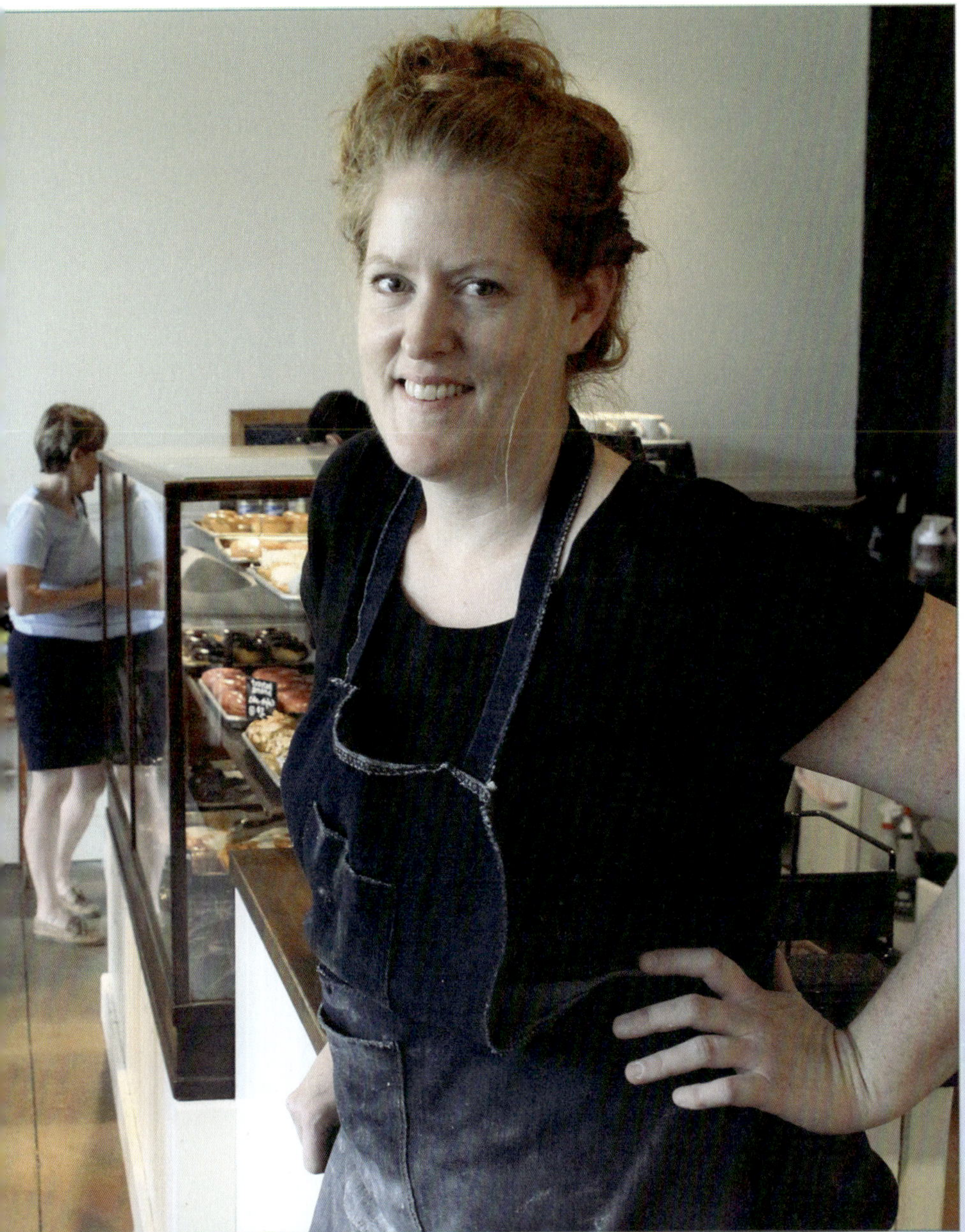

Maria Moore Riggs, owner of Revolution Doughnuts in Decatur, Georgia, used Kickstarter to help fund her storefront when she went through most of her savings.

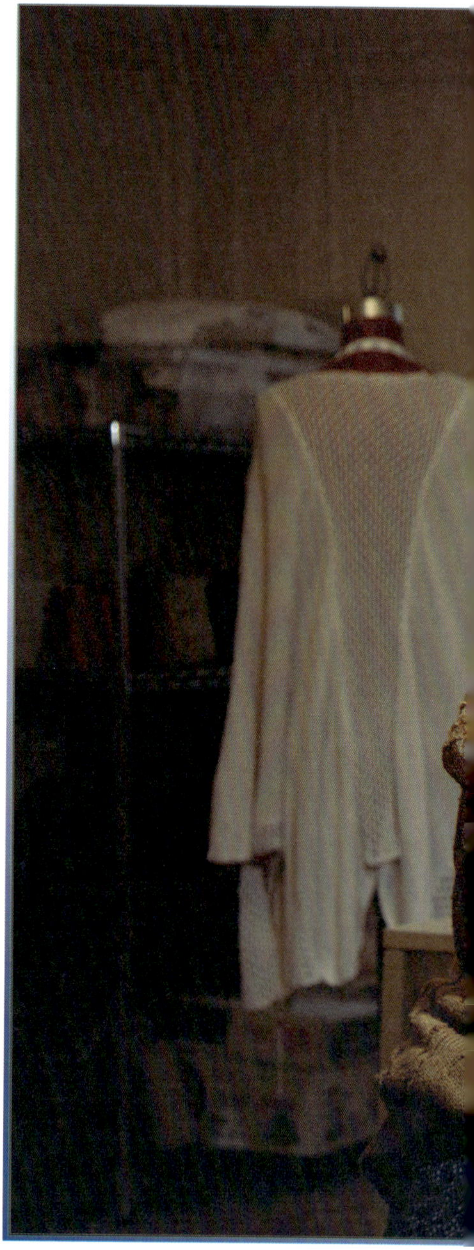

Two categories that don't get as much attention as the others are food and fashion.

In the food category, a device called the Nomiku has been the most successful, raising $586,000. The item cooks meat sous-vide, which is a method of cooking in water in sealed, airtight plastic bags. But products have included artisan hot sauces, cocktail bitters, cupcakes infused with alcohol, vegan ice cream, beer cookies, cookbooks, and distilleries.

Fashion projects also don't get as much attention as some of the other categories. Strickler has said in the *New York Times* that fashion projects can take a storefront approach where a designer puts forward prototypes. Some of these projects have included a line of mountain bike clothing for women. With other fashion programs, a supporter may not be preordering anything but helping fund a line

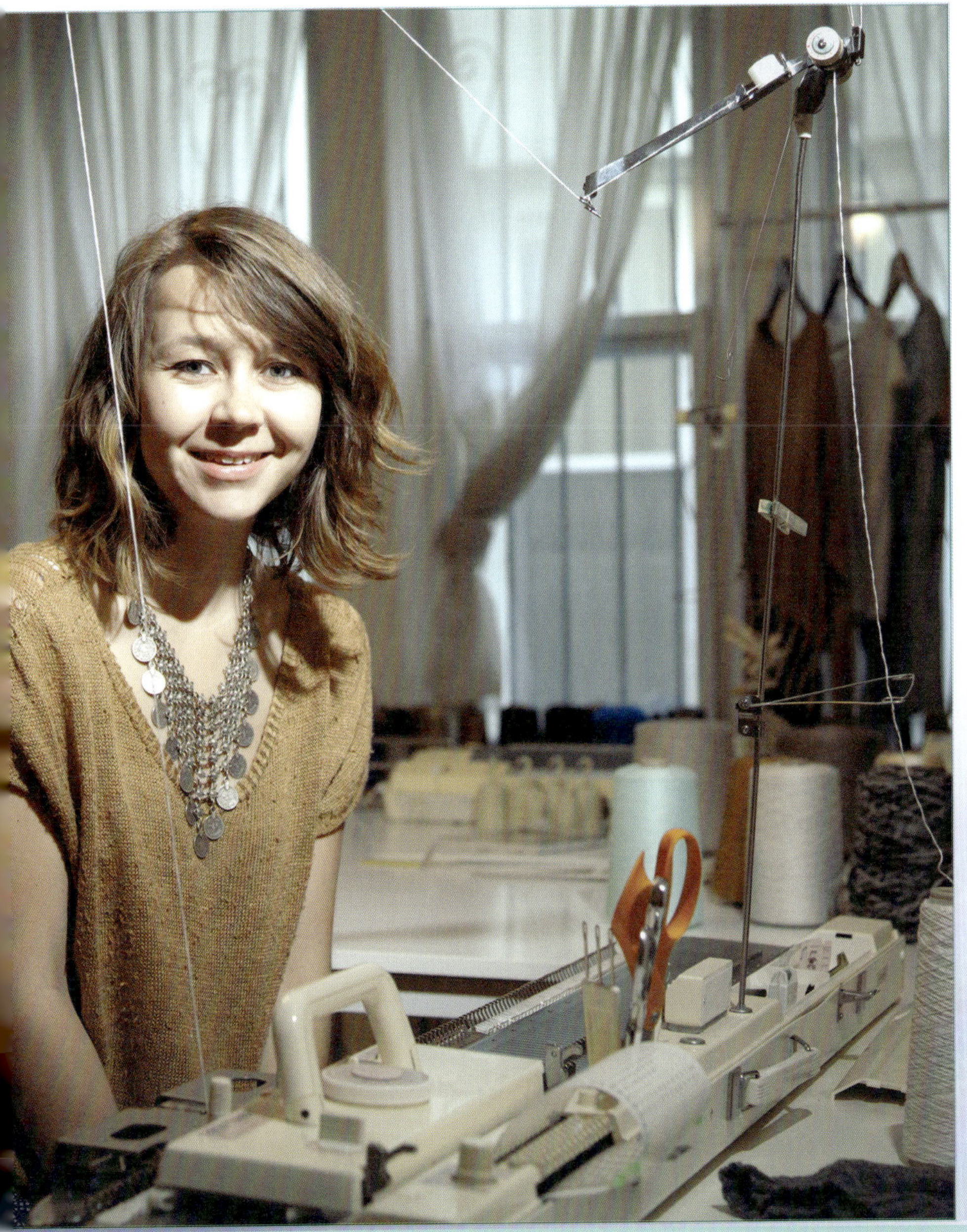

Kickstarter has proven to be an effective fund-raising tool for emerging fashion designers like Brooklyn-based Mandy Kordal, who is launching a line of knitwear.

from a designer. The reward may be spending time with the designer or getting a personally designed T-shirt.

MAKING MORE CREATIVE CHANNELS

One of the ways Kickstarter has kept interesting projects coming through its pipeline is by curating pages with artistic organizations. It has given the Sundance Institute, Rhode Island School of Design, New Museum, and Pitchfork special space on its site to spotlight crowdfunded projects started by people connected to those organizations. They have a staff member now who is dedicated to seeking out talent and helping them develop ideas that could be supported via Kickstarter.

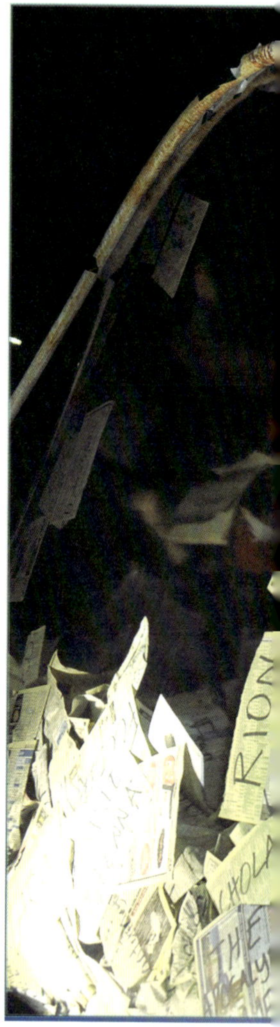

Although tech projects have brought in a lot of money for Kickstarter, the most money raised over Kickstarter's history has come from film and video, followed by music and design. The most successful category has been dance, followed by theater and music.

NEW HORIZONS, NEW PROBLEMS

Throughout its three-year history, Kickstarter has dealt strictly in the United States. Shortly after it turned three, however, Strickler and Chen announced plans to expand to England. Kickstarter has been unable to cater to international projects because Amazon Payments would work only with U.S. bank accounts. In 2011, Amazon Payments expanded into England.

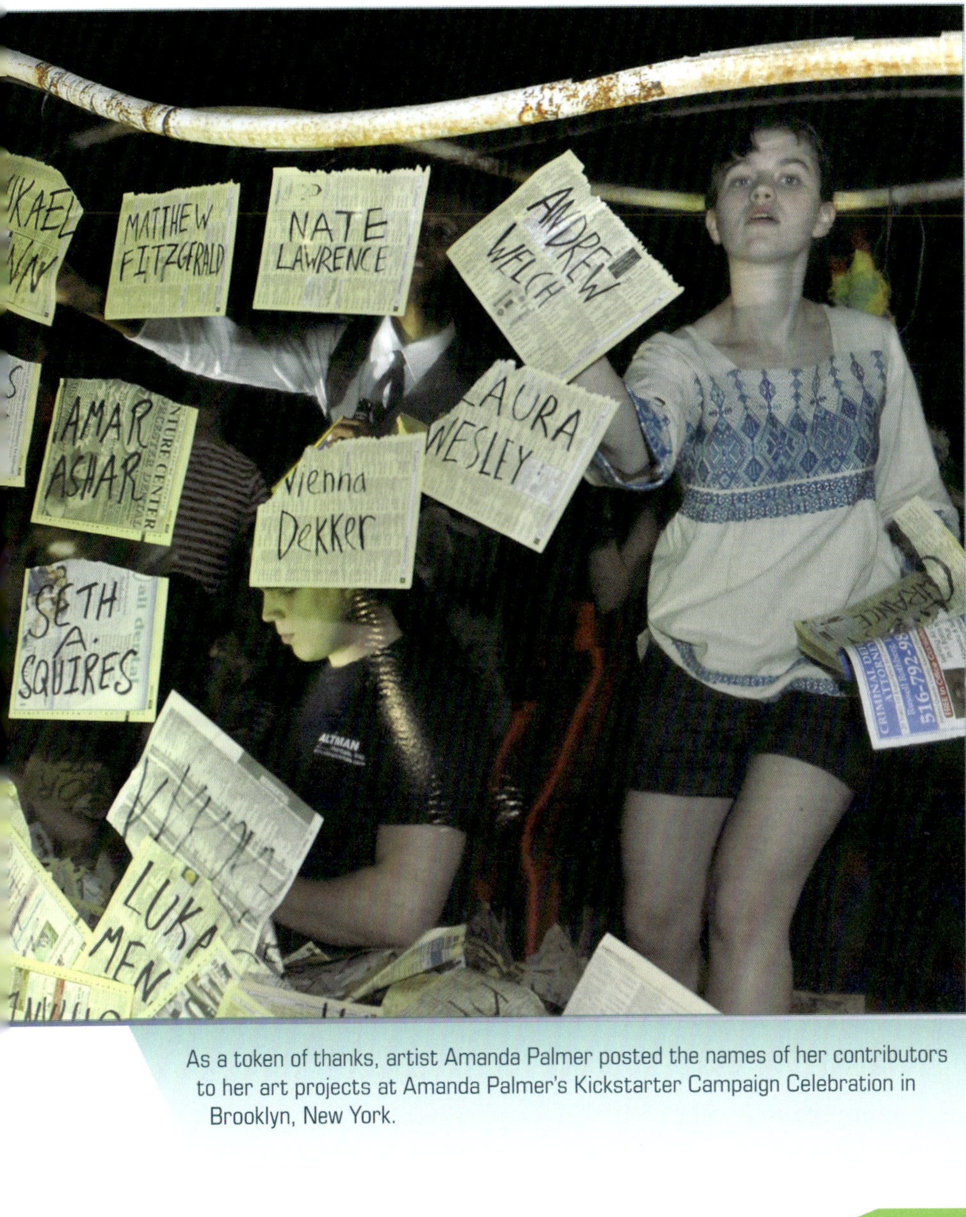

As a token of thanks, artist Amanda Palmer posted the names of her contributors to her art projects at Amanda Palmer's Kickstarter Campaign Celebration in Brooklyn, New York.

In August, Kickstarter announced a new feature: the backer info card. This feature gives project creators a snapshot of who its financial backers are. Clicking it reveals how much the backer pledged, when their pledge was made, which reward they selected, and any notes the creator has made about them.

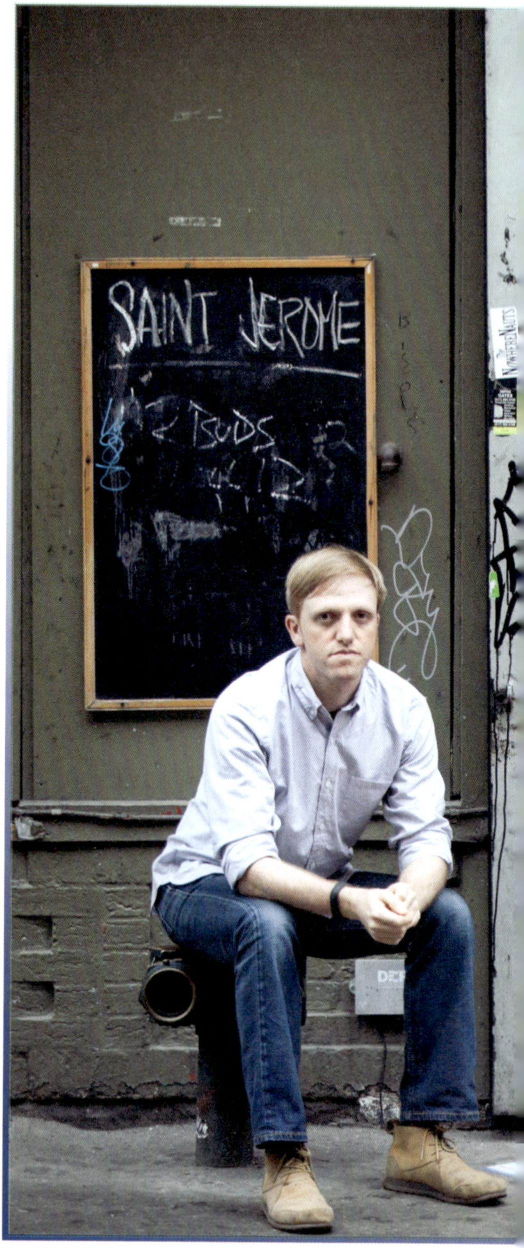

Chen said that they are working on the tools to make finding projects that interest users easier. Kickstarter doesn't have a mobile-friendly version or iPad app, but these are on the list for future endeavors. Chen is concerned about fraud and security issues as well. Ultimately, though, he said that they depend on users to police the site and tell them when something is off.

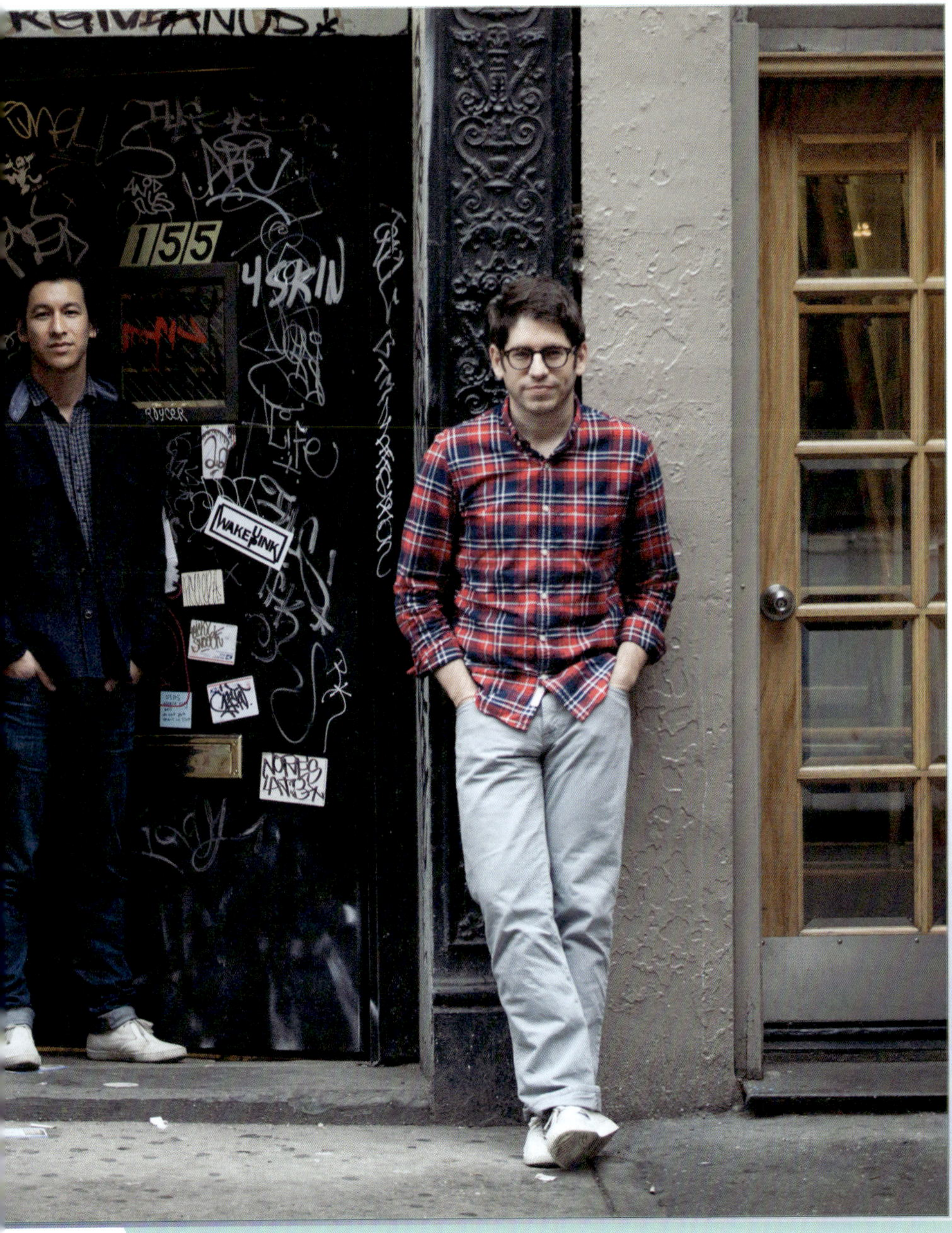

Adler, Chen, and Strickler have created a multimillion-dollar business in a few short years. In the years ahead, they plan to expand to Great Britain and beyond.

One of the issues that isn't brought up often is the fact that money raised through crowdfunding is income, and those who receive funding may need to pay taxes on such funds. A report filed by Bernadette Tansey on CNBC mentioned that Kickstarter revenue minus expenses could be seen as taxable profit. But the issue of taxes has not been raised much in Kickstarter circles. In an article in *Forbes* magazine, Jamie Sutherland, president of accounting software Xero's U.S. operations, said that he felt many people, including accountants, hadn't fully grasped the significance of crowdfunding: "The tax implications for crowdfunded 'income' are probably not that well understood by the average startup. I'd encourage a startup to connect with a knowledgeable accountant or tax adviser so they can fully understand their tax obligations"

In the summer of 2012, the Kickstarter blog stressed that it was still the site for the small investor, and it posted how contributing just $1 can still really make a difference. Earlier in 2012, Amanda Palmer set a Kickstarter record by having 4,743 people pledge to her $1 reward. Those who chipped in just $1 received a digital download of her new album. In addition to one of the creators of *Penny Arcade* promising to shout your name while chasing a duck, there have been some other great perks for $1 donations. A fund-raiser for a painting depicting comic and video game characters promised to include your suggestion for a character that absolutely had to be included.

The idea that people can all chip in as little as $1 to make a creative project come alive has been at the core of what Kickstarter is all about. Chen, the former waiter who now leads a multimillion dollar crowdfunding site, recognizes that things have changed since the site began. However, as Chen has said on GigaOm: "We honestly don't really care if we have million-dollar projects. We're just interested in projects."

Fact Sheet on

Perry Chen

Age: Thirty-five

Birthplace: New York, New York

Education: Tulane University and Hong Kong University of Science and Technology

Previous Job(s): Waiter, gallery owner

Current Residence: New York City

Current Title: Cofounder and CEO of Kickstarter

Marital Status: Single

Favorite City: Chen loves New Orleans and hopes to have an office there one day.

Net Worth: Unknown

Fact Sheet on

Yancey Strickler

Age: Thirty-three

Birthplace: Blacksburg, Virginia

Education: College of William and Mary

Previous Job(s): Music writer/editor

Current Residence: New York City

Current Title: Cofounder of Kickstarter

Marital Status: Single

Favorite Book: *All the President's Men*

Favorite Music: Big Black, Gang of Four, and the MC5, as well as the country sounds of the Flying Burrito Brothers, the Byrds, Doc Watson, Uncle Tupelo, and Wilco

Net Worth: Unknown

Fact Sheet on

Charles Adler

Age: Thirty-eight

Birthplace: Unavailable

Education: Studied mechanical engineering technology at Purdue University

First Job(s): Designer and Web site builder

Current Residence: New York City

Current Title: Creative director/Interaction designer/co-founder Kickstarter

Marital Status: Married

Favorite Activities: Cycling, running, snowboarding, golfing, fishing, camping, hiking

Net Worth: Unknown

Fact Sheet on KICKSTARTER

Founded: April 28, 2009

Slogan: "Fund and Follow Creativity." Kickstarter is a funding platform for creative projects.

Original Name: Kickstartr

Founders: Perry Chen, Yancey Strickler, and Charles Adler

Headquarters: New York City

Number of Employees: 40

Launched Projects: 69,031

Dollars Pledged to All Projects: $337 million

Pledges Collected: $283 million

Success Rate of Kickstarter Projects: 44 percent

Value: $3.21 million

Timeline

2002 Perry Chen thinks of the idea for Kickstarter when trying to stage a concert in New Orleans.

2005 Perry Chen meets Yancey Strickler at Diner in Brooklyn, New York. He shares the idea with Strickler, and they agree to develop the business together.

2007 Chen and Strickler meet Charles Adler and bring him on as third team member to help with design and technical aspects of Kickstarter.

2008 Kickstarter creates models for its Web site.

2009 On April 28, the team launches Kickstarter.

2010 On December 16, iPod Nano watch project called the TikTok reaches $942,578.

Kickstarter becomes recognized as a way to launch products.

Time magazine declares Kickstarter one of the fifty best inventions of 2010.

2011 Kickstarter averages $1million a week in pledges at the beginning of the year.

Kickstarter receives almost $100 million in pledges, more than tripling the dollar amount of pledges from 2010.

Kickstarter becomes the third-largest publisher of comics in America.

February 9, 2012 An iPod dock created by ElevationLab becomes the first project to ever get a million dollars on the site.

Spring 2012 Kickstarter announces plans to expand to the United Kingdom.

May 2012 In May, the Pebble Smartwatch surpasses $10 million in pledges.

Musician Amanda Palmer raises almost $1.2 million for her next recording, book, and tour.

August 2012 Ouya sets out to raise $950,000 to produce a hackable Android-based gaming console that would compete with PlayStation, Wii, and Xbox. The company raises $8.6 million, with a promise to deliver the product by March 2013.

Glossary

Android Google's open-source operating system designed to work on mobile devices.

angel investor An investor who gives financial backing for start-ups or entrepreneurs. Typically, they are more interested in helping the business succeed than reaping a large profit.

API (application programming interface) A set of programming instructions and routines for accessing an online software application or Web tool.

capital Money or goods used to generate income by investing in a business or in another type of income-making venture.

crowdfunding Asking a large group of people to give a defined amount of money for a specific project or cause in exchange for possible rewards.

first-person shooter (FPS) A game in which the player sees the action on screen as if he or she were the character.

game console An interactive entertainment computer or system specially designed to play computer games.

hacker A person who uses his or her computer knowledge to get unauthorized information or use of a system.

incentive A gift, service, or discount that motivates somebody to take action.

iPhone A line of Internet and multimedia-enabled smartphones designed and marketed by Apple.

iPod Nano An extra-small digital audio player designed and marketed by Apple.

Livestream A video platform that lets users watch and broadcast live video content over the Internet using a camera and computer.

microfinancing Closely related to crowdfunding, a financial model often used online to raise money or provide loans for low-income clients.

patronage Financial support or encouragement, often provided by a person or organization of wealth and given to an artist to pursue his or her creative endeavors.

platform An underlying computer system that allows applications to operate.

point-and-click game A graphic adventure computer game where the player must actively respond to commands on screen and advance the action by clicking on various images.

securities Financial instruments such as stocks or bonds. A security represents some type of financial value in a company or with a government body.

start-up A business or operation that is just beginning.

tweet A message of 140 characters or less sent through the social networking service Twitter.

venture capitalist An investor who provides funding for promising business ventures. Usually these businesses are start-ups. Venture capitalists invest with the intention of making a big profit by taking a financial risk.

For More Information

Canadian Advanced Technology Alliance (CATA)
207 Bank Street, Suite 416
Ottawa, ON K2P 2N2
Canada
(613) 236-6550
Web site: http://www.cata.ca
The largest high-tech association in Canada, CATA is a comprehensive resource for the latest high-tech news in Canada.

GetNetWise
Internet Education Foundation
1634 Eye Street NW
Washington, DC 20006
(202) 638-4370
Web site: http://www.getnetwise.org
GetNetWise is a public service sponsored by Internet industry corporations and public interest organizations dedicated to making sure that Internet users have positive, safe, and secure online experiences.

MediaSmarts
950 Gladstone Avenue, Suite 120
Ottawa, ON K1Y 3E6
Canada
(800) 896-3342
Web site: http://www.mediasmarts.ca
MediaSmarts is a Canadian nonprofit organization for digital and media literacy, with helpful resources on these subjects. MediaSmarts's work falls into the areas of education, public awareness, and research and policy.

New York Tech Meetup
175 Varick Street
New York, NY 10014
Web site: http://www.nytm.org
Founded in 2004, NY Tech Meetup has nearly 26,000 members, made up of professionals from all parts of the New York technology community. (You must be eighteen to join.) The organization sponsors monthly events featuring talks and product demos and has been central to the rebirth of New York's Silicon Alley.

OpenMedia
1424 Commercial Drive
P.O. Box 21674
Vancouver, BC V5L 5G3

Canada
(604) 633-2744
Web site: http://www.openmedia.ca
OpenMedia is a Canadian grassroots organization that safeguards the possibilities of the open and affordable Internet.

Young Entrepreneur
Entrepreneur Media Inc.
2445 McCabe Way, Suite 400
Irvine, CA 92614
(949) 261-2325
Web site: http://www.youngentrepreneur.com
Launched in 1999, Young Entrepreneur is one of the largest online forum communities for entrepreneurs worldwide. The site includes a blog, how-to articles, and the latest entrepreneurial news and information.

WEB SITES

Due to the changing nature of Internet links, Rosen Publishing has developed an online list of Web sites related to the subject of this book. This site is updated regularly. Please use this link to access the list:

http://www.rosenlinks.com/IBIO/Kick

For Further Reading

Crowder, David. *Building a Web Site for Dummies.* Hoboken, NJ: Wiley Publishing, 2010.

Farrell, Mary. *Computer Programming for Teens*. Boston, MA: Thomas Course Technology, 2008.

Freedman, Jeri. *Careers in Computer Science and Programming*. New York, NY: Rosen Classroom, 2011.

Goldsworthy, Steve. *Steve Jobs* (Remarkable People). New York, NY: AV2 by Weigl, 2011.

Grant, Michael. *BZRK*. New York, NY: Egmont, 2012.

Hansen, Mark Victor. *The Richest Kids in America: How They Earn It, How They Spend It, How You Can Too.* Newport Beach, CA: Hansen House, 2009.

Ivester, Mark. *LOL...OMG!: What Every Student Needs to Know About Online Reputation Management, Digital Citizenship and Cyberbullying*. Reno, NV: Serra Knight Publishing, 2011.

Lawton, Kevin, and Dan Marom. *The Crowdfunding Revolution: Social Networking Meets Venture Financing*. Self-published: CreateSpace, 2010.

Livingston, Jessica. *Founders at Work: Stories of Startups' Early Days*. Berkeley, CA: APRESS, 2007.

Lloyd, Ian. *Build Your Own Web Site the Right Way Using HTML & CSS*. 2nd ed. Collingwood, Australia: Site Point Pty, 2008.

Lusted, Marcia Amidon. *Mark Zuckerberg: Facebook Creator* (Essential Lives). Edina, MN: Abdo Publishing Company, 2012.

Lusted, Marcia Amidon. *Social Networking: MySpace, Facebook, & Twitter* (Technology Pioneers). Edina, MN: Abdo Publishing Company, 2012.

Marques, Marcelo. *Hackerteen: Volume 1: Internet Blackout*. Sebastopol, CA: O'Reilly, 2009.

Rankin, Kenrya, and Eriko Takada. *Start It Up: The Complete Teen Business Guide to Turning Your Passions Into Pay*. San Francisco, CA: Zest Books, 2011.

Sethi, Maneesh. *Game Programming for Teens*. Boston, MA: Course Technology, 2009.

Steinberg, Don. *The Kickstarter Handbook: Real Life Success Stories of Artists, Inventors, and Entrepreneurs*. Philadelphia, PA: Quirk Books, 2012.

Steinberg, Scott. *The Crowdfunding Bible: How to Raise Money for Any Startup, Video Game, or Project*. Self-published: Read.me, 2012.

Swartz, Jon. *Young Wealth: Trade Secrets from Teens Who Are Changing American Business*. Bloomington, IN: Rooftop Publishing, 2006.

Bibliography

Adler, Carlye. "How Kickstarter Became a Lab for Daring Prototypes and Ingenious Products." *Wired*, March 18, 2011. Retrieved September 4, 2012 (http://www.wired.com/magazine/2011/03/ff_kickstarter).

Allen, Todd. "Web Comic Raises 1.25 Million on Kickstarter." *Publishers Weekly*, February 21, 2012. Retrieved September 4, 2012 (http://www.publishersweekly.com).

Calacanis, Jason. "Interview with Yancey Strickler." *Startups*, "#151" on YouTube, June 24, 2011. Retrieved September 4, 2012 (http://www.youtube.com).

Details. "2010 Mavericks: Yancey Strickler, Perry Chen, John Auerbach & Chris Wong." October 2010. Retrieved September 4, 2012 (http://www.details.com).

Franzen, Carl. "Kickstarter Expects to Provide More Funding to the Arts Than NEA." Talking Points Memo, February 24, 2012. Retrieved September 4, 2012 (http://idealab.talkingpointsmemo.com).

Harris, Jessica. "From Scratch: Yancey Strickler, Co-founder of Kickstarter." NPR, August 18, 2011. Retrieved September 23, 2012 (http://www.npr.org).

Henderson, J. Maureen. "Is the Crowdfunding Bubble About to Burst?" *Forbes*, July 24, 2012. Retrieved September 4, 2012 (http://www.forbes.com).

Malik, Om. "Kickstarted: My Conversation with Kickstarter Co-founder Perry Chen." Gigaom.com, May 22, 2012. Retrieved September 4, 2012 (http://www.gigaom.com).

Mercer, Sam. "Kickstarter.com—An Interview with Co-Founder Yancey Strickler." PurplePawn.com, January 15, 2012. Retrieved September 4, 2012 (http://www.purplepawn.com).

Newton, Casey. "How the Pebble Became a Kickstarter Success Story." *San Francisco Chronicle*, April 28, 2012. Retrieved September 4, 2012 (http://www.sfgate.com).

Schiff, Lisa. "Kickstarter: Funding Creativity." *Huffington Post*, October 13, 2010. Retrieved September 4, 2012 (http://www.huffingtonpost.com).

Schragin, Adam. "Kickstart My Heart: Austin Figures Prominently in Kickstarter's Risks and Rewards." *Austin Chronicle*, February 24, 2012. Retrieved September 4, 2012 (http://www.austinchronicle.com).

Sisario, Ben. "Kickstarter Campaign Puts Amanda Palmer Over the Top." Telegram.com, June 7, 2012. Retrieved September 4, 2012 (http://www.telegram.com).

Snow, Kater. "Rock Center with Brian Williams." NBC, December 27, 2011. Retrieved September 23, 2012 (http://rockcenter.nbcnews.com).

Tolentino, Mellisa. "Three Years of Kickstarter: A Rewarding History." SiliconANGLE.com, May 14, 2012. Retrieved September 4, 2012 (http://www.siliconangle.com).

Vinh, Khoi. "An Interview with Charles Adler of Kickstarter." Subtraction.com, June 28, 2012. Retrieved September 4, 2012 (http://www.subtraction.com).

Walker, Rob. "The Trivialities and Transcendence of Kickstarter." *New York Times*, August 5, 2011. Retrieved September 4, 2012 (http://www.nytimes.com).

Wortham, Jenna. "A Few Dollars at a Time, Patrons Support Artists on the Web." *New York Times*, August 24, 2009. Retrieved September 4, 2012 (http://www.nytimes.com).

Index

K

L

M

N

O

P

R

S

T

U

W

Y

ABOUT THE AUTHOR

Don Rauf has a passion for new technology. He was the editor of the e-newsletter *Student Health 101*, which featured many state-of-the-art interactive elements and videos. He also authored *Killer Lipstick and Other Spy Gadgets*, about spy technology. He has cowritten several books with his wonderful wife, Monique Vescia.

PHOTO CREDITS

Cover, pp. 3, 11, 17 Taylor Hill/FilmMagic/Getty Images; p. 7 © iStockphoto.com/SeanShot; pp. 12–13 Timothy Hiatt/WireImage/Getty Images; pp. 14–15 Graham Crouch/Lonely Planet Images/Getty Images; p. 20 Karl Walter/Getty Images; pp. 24–25 Matteo Prandoni/BFAnyc/Sipa USA/Newscom; p. 29 DEA Picture Library/Getty Images; p. 31 Hulton Archive/Getty Images; pp. 36–37 Michael Nagle/The New York Times/Redux; p. 43 © Greg Sorber/Albuquerque Journal/ZUMA Press; p. 47 Jason Merritt/FilmMagic/Getty Images; pp. 48–49 Leah Nash/The New York Times/Redux; pp. 52–53 © The Toronto Star/ZUMA Press; p. 56 Dimitrios Kambouris/WireImage/Getty Images; p. 60 © AP Images; pp. 62–63 Travis Dove/The New York Times/Redux; p. 65 Anna Webber/Getty Images; pp. 70–71 Jim Wilson/The New York Times/Redux; p. 76 Bloomberg/Getty Images; pp. 82–83 David Goldman/The New York Times/Redux; pp. 84–85 © iStockphoto.com/Sam Burt Photography; pp. 88–89 Henry S. Dziekan III/WireImage/Getty Images; pp. 92–93 Larry Busacca/WireImage/Getty Images; pp. 98–99 © Phil Skinner/Atlanta Journal-Constitution/MCT/ZUMA Press; p. 100–101 Deidre Schoo/The New York Times/Redux; pp. 102–103 Jude Domski/Getty Images; pp. 104–105 James Estrin/The New York Times/Redux; background image pp. pp. 22, 38, 39, 50, 66, 67, 80, 81, 97 kentoh/Shutterstock.com; cover and remaining interior background image dpaint/Shutterstock.com.

Designer: Brian Garvey; Editor: Nicholas Croce;
Photo Researcher: Karen Huang